Communes in Britain

ANDREW RIGBY

ROUTLEDGE & KEGAN PAUL
London and Boston

First published in 1974
by Routledge & Kegan Paul Ltd
Broadway House, 68–74 Carter Lane,
London EC4V 5EL and
9 Park Street,
Boston, Mass. 02108, USA
Set in 10 on 12 point Monotype Modern Extended No. 7
and printed in Great Britain by
Clarke, Doble & Brendon Ltd, Plymouth
© Andrew Rigby 1974

ISBN 0 7100 7906 0 (C)
0 7100 7915 X (P)
Library of Congress Catalog Card No. 74–79361

Contents

Chapter 1

Introduction

Most observers of the social scene would agree that over the last decade significant changes have been taking place in the relationships between pre- and post-war generations in the industrialised societies of the West. For some reason or other, and the reasons put forward as explanations differ according to the age and political stance of the alleged theorist, generations born since the war seem less committed than their parents to the practice of nine till five work-a-day living, the idea of pursuing a steady career, of planning for the future, of saving money for the rainy days of the future, of 'getting ahead' in terms of possessing money, property and consumer goods. More generally, there seems to be, on the part of many sectors of the population but particularly the young, a serious questioning of traditional, taken-for-granted assumptions about the way individual and social group life should be led. It is as though people now want something more out of life than a guarantee that somehow or other they will get the cash to feed themselves and their family for the week. Perhaps at its simplest this general change in people's attitudes merely reflects the concern of increasing numbers of people to actually *enjoy* their lives.

The spread of this disaffection from the 'straightness' of the capitalist societies has led many people to believe that a general revolutionary movement is developing, one which has been variously labelled by observers and participants as the counter-culture, the underground, and more recently as 'conscious III'.[1] This movement lacks any well-defined objectives and goals other than a shared concern on the part of its participants to transform their own lives and that of straight society, to create an alternative social order characterised by values counter to those that appear to dominate our present existence. To the value of competitive individualism they counterpose the values of co-operation and brotherhood between people; against the values of conformity and routine they seek to establish that of creative individuality; to the belief in man's sovereign right to exploit nature for his own short-term instrumental purposes they seek to present the image of 'mother earth' in whose family man in only one of the many life forms that she sustains and whom we must respect and love if life is to persist. They seek to subvert the sacred respect and obeisance paid to 'experts' by proclaiming the right of each individual to have a voice in the control of his own environment and living space. They seek to replace parliamentary democracy by new forms of decision-making involving the devolution of power, and to replace the capitalist system of production for profit, sustained by artificially stimulated demands, by a system of production for use in order to meet genuine needs—the list could go on.

Such ideas and images, however, tend to be vague and unstructured, and consequently the actions directed by such visions tend to be hesitant and uncertain. Amongst the activities and projects developed by the 'partisans' of this general movement, however, one can refer to the growth of free schools and centres for experiments in the arts, the spread of the squatters movements, the attempts to develop community action groups and tenants' associations, the mushrooming of branches of the Claimants' Union throughout Britain, the emergence of underground papers and publications,[2] along with the specific movements for Women's Liberation and Gay Liberation. All these represent the attempts of people who perceive a gap between the way life *is* and the way they feel life *ought to be,* and who seek to transform their own lives and that of society in general towards their ideal; the attempts of people to implement in the here-and-now those values which they hope to see adopted on a societal-wide scale in the future.

One of the specific arms of this general counter-cultural movement is the Commune Movement. Like the general movement, this is trans-national in its dimensions. Recent years have seen the growth of communal ventures in many countries of the world, but mainly in the industrialised West. It is incredibly difficult to estimate the number of communes in any one country. Many groups hide from the light of publicity, fearing the inevitable flood of visitors that would result.

Other groups have a very short life together, perhaps only of a few months. New groups form themselves into communes whilst others cease to exist. There is no official census of such living experiments and, anyway, what is a commune?

A formal definition would be something along the following lines: a commune consists of a group of people, of three or more persons in size, drawn from more than one family or kinship group, who have voluntarily come together for some purpose or other, shared or otherwise, in the pursuit of which they seek to share certain aspects of their lives together, and who are characterised by a certain consciousness of themselves as a group. The sharing together of their lives may range across such dimensions as living accommodation, economic activities and income, child-rearing and perhaps also sexual activities. As will be seen in later chapters, different groups share their lives together to different degrees. With some there is sharing across all these dimensions, with others it is kept to the minimal level of sharing the same property as living accommodation. In fact, falling under the general term of 'commune' one encounters a whole variety of experiments in living and this makes it very difficult in one's attempts at definition to satisfy those who demand that their 'labels' be clear, concise, pure and uncomplicated. Due to the definitional difficulties, and also due to my dislike of the way many social scientists manage to distort the world through neatly allocating phenomena to particular categories without any concern for how the actual people involved on the 'ground floor', so to speak, define their activities, the definition that I worked with during my research into communes was a simple one—if a group of people living together considered themselves to be a commune, then I accepted their definition of themselves and treated them as such. In practice no group would be likely to define itself as a commune unless the members felt that they met, or would eventually meet, certain of the criteria mentioned above.

Given these problems about definitions, and bearing in mind the difficulties of making any accurate estimate of the actual number of communes in existence around the globe, some rough approximation of figures can be made. In the USA it was estimated that there were over 2,000 rural communes of one sort or another in existence in 1970.[3] This figure did not include all the many types of urban groups that were in existence. In Japan there are apparently some 50 communes and approximately 300 co-operative villages.[4] In

Israel the kibbutz movement has continued to grow to the point where there are over 235 kibbutzim with a total population of over 90,000, about 4 per cent of the Israeli Jewish population.[5] On the continent of Europe communes have sprung up in most of the major urban centres, inspired to some extent by the example of Kommune 1 which was founded in Berlin in the spring of 1967 and whose members received a great deal of attention through their political activities.[6] In Holland it has been estimated that there are over 200 community ventures run by members of the Roman Catholic Church.[7] In Britain the Commune Movement has sought to bring out an annual Directory of Communes listing those communal ventures that have come to the notice of the Movement. The 1971 issue listed some 40 ventures, but a more realistic estimate of the number of communes in existence in Britain in 1972 would be around the 100 mark.

In examining the different types of communes in existence one can rely on a number of possible criteria to distinguish between ventures. One can distinguish between rural and urban based projects. One could differentiate between groups according to the degree of sharing adhered to—thus many commentators save the term commune for those groups who share most aspects of their lives together, whilst using the term community for those character-ised by a fairly minimal level of co-operation, such as shared living accommodation. One could also classify communes according to size—one of the groups discussed in a later chapter has a resident membership of over 100 whilst most groups have about 6–12 mem-bers. Any attempt to categorise the different types of communes will involve some distortion and simplification of the actual reality, if only because communes change in their nature over time and each venture is a reflection of the unique nature of its members and its situation. However, some simplification is unavoidable if the unfamiliar reader is to gain some insight into the complexities of the commune scene—so that is my excuse and my apology for attempting to suggest a classificatory scheme into which communes can be 'slotted'.

Another term often used to refer to communes is that of 'inten-tional community'. What this term does indicate is the idea of people coming together to live for some conscious purpose or other, the idea that people are seeking to experiment with patterns of living for some reason. Different groups come together for different purposes, and since in their inception most communal groups have talked for some time about what they hope to achieve, there is a strong likelihood that in the early life of a group at least there will have emerged a shared conception of the purpose or the intention of the commune. Hence, the typology (or rather the list) of communes presented below is based upon the different intentions underlying different ventures. This does not exhaust the different types in any way, but it does cover most of the groups at present in existence in Britain, and from my reading on the subject of communes in the USA the use of this skeleton would not distort the reality of the commune scene there too much.

In an earlier work I suggested that communes could profitably be considered in terms of a six-fold typology.[8] This went as follows:

1 *Self-actualising communes* This label refers to those experiments in communal living that are seen by their members as contributing towards the creation of a new social order by providing, within the community, that environment in which individual members feel most free to discover their true selves, to extend their self-awareness, learn to develop their individual creative potentialities and realise true individual freedom within the context of a communal group.

2 *Communes for mutual support* These communes are typically seen by their members not only as contributing to the movement for social change, but also as important for the individual members, providing them with a setting of mutual support and a supportive environment within which they can discover a sense and feeling of brotherhood with the other members that they have been unable to discover in the world 'outside'.

3 *Activist communes* The members of this type of commune define the purpose of their project primarily in terms of providing an urban base from which they can directly involve themselves in 'outside' social and political activity of one sort or another.

4 *Practical communes* Whereas the members of the above types of commune would justify their experiment at least partly in terms of their commitment to bringing about radical social change, the members of practical communes define their venture primarily in terms of the economic and practical material advantages to be obtained through such a style of life. The saving on living costs is emphasised as the purpose of the commune rather than the creation of the alternative society, or whatever.

5 *Therapeutic communes* As the label implies, this sort of

commune is typically defined, at least by its founder members, as having the prime purpose of therapy. They are aimed above all at the creation of that social, physical and spiritual environment within which particular types of people who are considered to be in need of care and attention can be looked after, and prepared for what is considered to be a more rewarding kind of life, by the founder members, 'staff' or 'house workers' of the commune.

6   *Religious communes*   These are communes where the goal is defined by members primarily in religious terms. The commune is viewed as fulfilling some purpose or other which the members feel to be in accordance with their religious beliefs, a venture which they consider to be at least partly inspired and possibly guided by supra-empirical or sacred forces. Within this category I distinguished between two basic types according to the different types of religious belief system that appeared to inspire communal ventures. On the one hand it seemed that there were some ventures that were inspired by a belief in a transcendent deity, a 'God up there', and the desire to serve Him through seeking to resolve the conflict between His injunctions and the 'ways of the world' by living a life in accordance with God's Word within a community. In some contrast with such ascetic religious communes, the members of ventures guided by a mystic belief system believe in an immanent Divine Power that is within and throughout all things, and aspire to attain oneness with this universal force. As such the members of mystic religious communes are generally more concerned with cultivating their spiritual consciousness and awareness, rather than with the project of transforming worldly life in accordance with the dictates of the ascetic's transcendent God.

Of course no commune is founded in order to pursue or attain a single goal, and different members are obviously concerned to pursue their own individual projects which can vary within a commune membership, the goals of communes change with the passage of time. All this means that one should treat the typology above as a set of coat-hangers which happened to be useful to hang my observations upon in a previous work and which I have found useful in ordering my ideas and perceptions about communes since that time. However, a number of further qualifying remarks ought to be made.

First of all, it should be mentioned that whilst different communes are founded for different purposes, most members join ventures at least in part because of their felt need for mutual support. By the very fact that they are interested in new styles of living they show that they are disaffected from certain aspects of life as it is conventionally led in the West, whether this is merely a dislike of living in a Wimpey-style house or a total opposition to the capitalist system as a whole. In so far as their view of the world is somewhat different from that displayed by the bulk of their fellow men, then the position that they occupy is inevitably a problematic one, in that their commitment to their view of the world is constantly threatened by the refusal of others to recognise it as valid. Like any minority group, their view of life is questioned by the majority, and with time the members of the minority will begin to doubt the validity of their particular ideas in the face of criticism, ridicule, incredulity and the questioning of representatives of what can be termed the cognitive majority, unless they can in some way insulate themselves, to an extent, from such pressures to change their ways of thinking. One strategy involves the creation of communes within which radicals or cognitive deviants may maintain the plausibility of their knowledge. It can be argued that only through the creation of a strong sense of brotherhood and solidarity such as is possible within a community of 'believers' can the challenges of the cognitive antagonists be repelled. This is perfectly illustrated by the member of an activist commune in Edinburgh which will be considered in a later chapter, who wrote of how they had all come together as radical students at university and decided to form a communal venture on leaving college. She wrote:[9]

> The attitudes of the people in the group towards the idea of living communally are not all the same . . . some of us feel that, now that we are more exposed to the compromising forces of the broader social order, living in a group of like-minded people will help us to retain our ideological integrity and sustain an ongoing educative process.

Secondly, it should be borne in mind that religious communes in particular are frequently oriented towards the fulfilment of some purpose or other which is shared by secular ones, the only difference being that this purpose stems from the religious beliefs of the founder members rather than from secular beliefs. Thus the Camphill communities appear to be perfect examples of therapeutic communes in so far as they are oriented towards the care of children and adults suffering from mental, emotional and physical disturbances. At the same time, however, the therapeutic work that is carried on within such communities is based upon the body of knowledge of the physical and spiritual worlds developed by Rudolph Steiner and known as Anthroposophy. This belief system, with its emphasis on the divine inner core that is within each and every individual, the belief in reincarnation and karma, can be viewed as very closely akin to the mystic religious beliefs of the Orient. To the extent that the communities represent an attempt to create a life according to the knowledge passed on by Steiner, they can be viewed as religious communes. To the extent that the work is primarily oriented to the care of the handicapped, with the work of Steiner merely providing a useful source of guidance and advice with which to pursue this aim, they can be seen as therapeutic communes. In fact, most people involved with the Camphill communities would probably see the two aspects as inextricably linked. This illustrates the limitations of any attempt to construct a definitive typology of communal ventures if one is to remain open to the uniqueness of each individual experiment. This point will be returned to later.

Despite this variety of types of commune, is it possible to come to any worthwhile generalisations about why there should be this growth of new experiments in living in the present period? Social movements have been a favourite subject of study by sociologists for many years, and one of the foremost students of such phenomena has written that social movements[10]

> have their inception in a condition of unrest, and derive their motive power on the one hand from dissatisfaction with the current form of life, and on the other hand, from wishes and hopes for a new scheme or system of living.

Thus, in order to understand the growth of communes in contemporary society it is necessary first of all to locate the origins of the members' estrangement from the existing social order, the sources of their discontent with the *status quo*. However, it is not sufficient merely to ask and to try and answer the simple question, 'what aspects of contemporary life do commune members find particularly unbearable?' One must enquire further. One must ask the question 'Why?'—'Why do certain groups of people find different aspects of life in modern society unbearable, when other groups appear to find such conditions tolerable?'

The answers to such questions lie in the particular life problems encountered by members of particular social groups located in particular areas of the social structure. One cannot begin to understand the contemporary commune movement without taking account of the impact of certain social forces upon the structure of modern industrialised societies in general, and without considering how these social forces have had different consequences for the lives of members of different social groups in particular.

Thus, it is a common observation that the bulk of the commune membership is made up of young people drawn mainly from middle class social backgrounds. It can be argued that what has rendered increasing numbers of middle class youth available for recruitment to the commune movement has been what many people have termed the problem of personal identity. It can be argued that this experience, this inability to define oneself and to answer the basic questions of 'Who am I? What am I here for? Where am I going?' is a consequence of such forces as the high rate of technologically induced social change and the loss of traditional sources of personal identity and self-affirmation that has accompanied the development of large-scale, hierarchically organised institutions of economic, social and political life. What seems to have happened as a consequence of the forces of urbanisation, industrialisation, bureaucratisation and the centralisation of decision-making is that the power of such public institutions as the factory and the work place and the national polity over the individual has grown at the cost of those institutions concerned with the private areas of life (e.g. family, local community, and religion). It can be argued that the operations of such public institutions are increasingly dominated by norms and standards that are rational only in terms of the operation of the institution as a whole. Little concern is paid to the individual caught up in such organisations. Within them he has little opportunity to develop a meaningful sense of his own worth. He is treated more like the proverbial cog in the machine than an autonomous, thinking, conscious human being. As one writer has described the situation:[11]

Technology requires that man take on some of the characteristics of his tools, as well as vice versa. In a society dominated by technology, its logic—regularity which suppresses the idiosyncratic in favour of the predictable, the mechanization of time, the veneration of efficiency and output—stamps itself on the rest of society. All questions are ultimately decided by the experts, men whose final appeal is to science.

In the modern world the institutions shaping the individual's 'public life' have become restricted in their ability to provide meaning for the existence of the individual. At the same time there has been a corresponding decline in the significance of the institutions traditionally concerned with the individual's 'private' sphere of existence. There has been a decline in the relevance and significance of organised religion and its values as guidelines for the average individual's life style. As Alasdair MacIntyre has expressed it:[12]

> What the urbanization of the Industrial Revolution meant was the destruction of the older forms of community, in many cases rapidly, and in particular the destruction of those features of them to which religion had given symbolic expression. There is first of all the loss of a background of a given and largely unalterable social order within whose limits men of different social rank all have to live. There is secondly the disappearance of the relative continuity and stability of social order, a stability which makes that order appear continuous with the order of nature. There is thirdly an end to the existence of shared and established norms, common to all ranks in the community, in the light of which everyone stands either vindicated or convicted by their own conduct.

Whereas the individual is 'over-determined' in the primary public institutions and expected to play narrowly defined functionary roles, he is left to fend for himself in his private life. The decline of traditional communities, the high social and geographical mobility demanded of members of modern industrial society, the nature of the work task and the hours spent at work, the nature of the large, modern, anonymous urban and suburban communities—all these developments have meant that the individual in modern society can find it almost impossible to establish that network of intimate social relationships that are necessary if one is to gain reaffirmation through social interaction of one's sense of one's own inner worth as a human being.

This nature of 'man alone' helps to account for the materialism of the consumer culture. Promoted by the efforts of the advertising industry material goods become perceived as visible symbols of one's worth as a person. Material objects rather than fellow human beings are called upon to testify to one's worth. Unable to derive intrinsic satisfaction from his work task, unable to gain affirmation of his own worth through inter-personal relationships, unable to find solace in a religion whose traditional emphasis on brotherhood and love has become increasingly divorced from the competitive realities of economic life, increasingly separated from the centres of economic and political power and decision-making, and having had much of his sense of personal autonomy eroded by his experience of such events as the great economic depression and World War Two, the typical response of those born in the first third of this century has been a 'turning inward' on themselves and their immediate nuclear families. The typical response to the experience of being treated as small cogs in the big wheels of industry, polity and society has been to heed the wisdom of sticking to one's own business, leaving the complex problems of society alone, and focusing one's attention on the personal strategy of piloting oneself and one's family through the storm of life.

However, the representatives of other social groups can respond differently. Thus, for many young people, particularly from the middle class, who have been through the formal educational process of society and have become accustomed to think of themselves as worthy of respect as individuals, the prospect of such a life can appear as particularly repugnant. Especially so if they are aware that capitalist society now has the capabilities to satisfy our material needs and that the assumption of scarcity, that human needs can only be satisfied through participation in a competitive struggle for scarce resources with others, is a myth. As one writer has posed it: 'Why prepare if there will be so few satisfying jobs to prepare for? Why defer if there will be a super-abundance of inexpensively produced goods to choose from? Why plan if all plans can disintegrate into nuclear dust?'[13] The position of many young people then is that they are at a real loss as to what they should seek to become. They can perceive no attractive adult role models for them within the social structure. As a result certain of them are attempting to 'find themselves' and create a richer, more rewarding alternative style of life for themselves within the confines of a commune, concentrating on what one commune member has described as 'a life style in which work for money is irrelevant and undesired work is

B

minimised, thus permitting concentration on the objectives of developing every individual to his maximum capacity.[14]

The apparent rejection of society that the step of joining a commune implies can also be understood at least in part as a consequence of another development which typically accompanies rapid social change, the breakdown of what can be termed the 'institutionalisation of hypocrisy'. That is, every society is characterised by a discrepancy between the actual everyday practices of its members and the dominant ideals to which lip-service is piously paid by these same members. There develops a common-sense stock of knowledge about when and where it is 'reasonable' to expect people to adhere strictly to certain central values, such as 'Thou shalt not kill', and when and where it is 'unreasonable' to hold such expectations, such as in times of war. Young members of society are expected to become familiar with and to internalise such examples of the taken-for-granted hypocrisy of everyday life. However, in times of rapid social change this institutionalisation of hypocrisy can break down. New situations and practices emerge, with the result that the areas of 'value-exemption' have not had time to be defined and generally accepted. The universal gap between principle and practice appears with unusual clarity at such times, particularly to the young who have to some extent been shielded from this phenomenon within the confines of educational institutions where they have been instilled with the dominant values of the society. This perception is one of the most common sources of youthful radicalism, and one of the responses to such experiences is to seek to join or form a commune.

In the light of these observations, it does not seem so surprising that for many young people in contemporary society the transition from youth to conventional adulthood appears as either extremely problematic or downright undesirable. Given the unattractiveness or irrelevance of many adult role models available, given the apparent moral corruption and hypocrisy of capitalist society, and given the fact that many of today's youth want something more out of life than material success, particularly if they have tasted the fruits of such success within their homes—given these factors, then it is not too surprising that many young people, and those who identify with the young, are relatively available for recruitment to movements which appear to present possible solutions to their personal identity problems and their estrangement from the existing order of society.

But, of course, not all young people join communes, just as not all people in communes are those born since the last World War. Thus, in order to discover why the minority do choose to form or join a commune it is necessary to enquire into their personal biographies. It is necessary to trace the paths pursued by individuals which have led them to a communal way of life. For this task the concept of the 'career' can be used, as it has been done by others, to refer to[15]

> any social strand of any person's course through life. The perspective of natural history is taken: unique outcomes are neglected in favour of such changes over time as are basic and common to the members of a social category, although occurring independently to each of them.

Thus, it is possible to argue that for any individual to join a commune he must first feel dissatisfied with at least certain aspects of his life in conventional society. Furthermore, he must become aware that such phenomena as communes exist in the world. Third, he must have had some experience which has caused him to think that such a style of life might be agreeable to people like himself. He must also become aware that particular communes are in existence at the present time where he believes he may be able to discover an environment amenable to the pursuance of his own personal goals. He must in addition establish contact with such communes by some means or other in order for him to gain acceptance as a member. Finally, and perhaps more crucially, he must define his own situation as sufficiently free for him to change his way of living and commence a new life. If a person is unable to discover any existing communes that fit his particular vision or is unable to gain admission to one, then he must attempt by some means or other to contact others who share his dream and who are sufficiently committed to it and possess sufficient resources to translate this dream into reality. To remain as a member of a commune a person must view his life there as sufficiently rewarding in various ways as to outweigh whatever possible advantages he might derive from returning to a more conventional mode of living. It is possible for any potential communard to 'drop out' or 'move off the path' to a commune at any one of these various points, just as it is possible to trace the paths pursued by those who actually do get to join a commune through these stages. The various paths to communes will be discussed in the ensuing chapters.

Of course it is one thing to become interested in communes and maybe join one, but it is a vastly different matter when you have to start from scratch and gather a group of people around you to join in your venture, and then keep the commune together if and when you have managed to launch your project. Indeed, on the basis of my experience it can be asserted that only a small fraction of communal ventures get beyond the embryo stage of planning to their implementation in practical living. Many aspiring commune members have failed to confront the problems actually involved in communal living because the obstacles facing those who are seeking to initiate such experiments have defeated them. Such problems are mainly of a two-fold nature. First of all there is the economic problem involved in raising the necessary capital to finance the venture, and the related problem of finding property of a suitable size, location, design, and cost to house the experiment. The other range of obstacles centre on the problems involved in gathering together a sufficient number of committed people with the necessary skills and resources to form the nucleus of the project.

Different communes face these problems in different measures. Just as it is possible to trace typical careers of commune members, so it is possible to trace different career patterns of communes themselves from the planning stage to that of practical implementation. Basically, one can distinguish three ideal-typical careers. The first involves those projects made up of a group of people who have been brought together because they share a common view of the world, a shared political and social or religious philosophy, which has led them to seek to form a commune. The second involves those who do not consciously share any firmly articulated set of beliefs but who are joined together primarily by bonds of friendship, these bonds being between the members as individuals rather than between them as 'believers'. The third involves those whose group identity is based on bonds of friendship between them as individuals and also upon their awareness of a shared faith in a particular belief system.

With regard to the first type, the letter columns of journals such as *Communes*, the journal of the Commune Movement in Britain, are full of letters from people seeking to join a particular form of communal venture or from people who are looking for certain sorts of people to join them in forming their own project. The chances of such people getting their venture off the ground would appear to be very slim. Not only do they face the economic problems that face others, but they also face the problem that their knowledge of each other is limited to an awareness that they share certain beliefs in common. They have never spent any amount of time in each other's company sufficient for them to form a sure opinion of the others as to their trustworthiness and for them to assuage their doubts about their ability to live communally together. If a commune is to get off the ground one of the minimal requirements is that all the potential members know and trust each other and are willing to face the prospect of living together. However, such trust and knowledge of each other can be obtained by no other way than actually spending a great deal of time in each other's company in a variety of situations. This is possible if the fellow believers all live within sufficiently close geographical proximity to each other for them to 'try each other out', but if they are separated by any degree of physical distance then it is very difficult to attain this level of intimate knowledge of each other without going to great expense in travel costs, trouble in terms of arranging holidays to suit each other, and so on. Usually the crunch comes with such groups when some of them eventually find property which they feel would be suitable for the group. People can talk for ages about what they will do when they get their commune but when the moment of decision comes, when they are faced with the prospect of acting *now*, giving up their old life to enter an experiment in living along with others about whom they feel they know only a limited amount—then it takes a brave person to make that final step, particularly if they have a felt responsibility to other members of their family and if they are called upon to make some sizeable financial contribution towards the scheme.

Those who come together in a commune as friends, before all else, typically pursue a different path. In fact their path often seems one that unintentionally leads to the commune. Such people have come together to live as a group purely on the basis that they like each other's company and without any specific philosophy about communes as such. Typically, such groups come together initially because they want to live together with their friends and because it is anticipated that such an arrangement would, amongst other things, reduce daily living costs. Thus, in a paradoxical way, whereas the economic problems are frequently those that defeat the plans of other groups, in the case of those 'unintentional communards' who come together as friends, it is their economic problems as individuals that have often led to the formation of the venture. Typically, such groups only come to think of themselves as a commune after they have been labelled as such by visitors and outsiders. This causes them to think about their style of group living, adopt the idea of themselves as a commune and then start thinking about where they are at as a communal group and what 'being a commune' actually means for them.

The economic problems are those which usually defeat the projects of people who, together, constitute the nucleus of a potential commune by virtue of their friendship and by the fact that these bonds are strengthened by a shared belief system and desire to live together as a commune. This problem of raising the necessary capital to obtain a place can tax the imagination of those who possess no savings, either through their past rate of expenditure or, as is more typical, through their reluctance to take on regular, paid, full-time employment. The member of one group consisting of 'nine artists, potters, designers and land lovers' described how they[16]

> found a large farm house and filled in an application for it. We were turned down. We are now collecting funds (our total joke bank account now stands at £2), money is a problem. Next week we will sell our bodies to the national health. We are collecting junk for a jumble sale but long-haired people don't have much jumble given to them, though friends have been over-generous to the jumble. We also have all the furniture we need and no house to put it in, nomadic and penniless we may be but we will succeed in our aim. Our dateline is July, we're in a hurry.

Despite their hurry, the members of this group eventually went their separate ways, as inevitably happens if such groups are not successful in obtaining property within a reasonable length of time. With the passage of the months people begin to lose faith that the venture will ever get off the ground, they begin to drift off pursuing other paths and eventually only the hard-core of maybe two or three people are left with their dreams, a little more wisdom and little else.

Despite such problems in getting a commune started, which defeat many groups, others persevere and are successful in finding property and gathering around them fellow communards. However, the reality of communal living can be somewhat harsher than was anticipated in the hazy days of planning and dreaming. Generally speaking, the 'problematic' areas of communal life relate first of all to the potential sources of conflict and dissension *within* the commune, and second to the sources of conflict between the commune and the wider society in general and the state in particular.

The founder of a religious community in the nineteenth-century USA argued that for a community to enjoy long life the members[17]

> should place all the power in the hands of their leader, and solemnly promise him unhesitating trust and obedience; specifying only that he should contract no debts, should attempt no new enterprise without unanimous consent, and should at all times open his purposes and his acts to the whole society.

Where a commune has been founded and is directed by a single leader who is respected by all the members of the group, whose word is accepted as final in any dispute that might occur, then such groups are likely to enjoy a relatively long life. Thus, a commune has been in existence in west London for over twenty years and now has a membership of nearly 100. It was founded by a psychotherapist who gathered around her friends and ex-patients with whom she sought to prove that people could live together in peace. This lady, who is now in her seventies, holds the love and respect of all the members, so that whenever dissent and problems emerge within the group it is her voice, based upon her long experience and knowledge, which is listened to and which contributes to the resolution of the difficulties. Similarly, one of the ventures in communal living considered in some detail in a later chapter has been directed for the first nine years of its life by the husband and wife team who founded the centre. The wife can appeal for advice from God whenever any problem arises and God's Will as revealed to her is translated into the practical realm through her husband. All the members accept these two as the leaders of the group not only because their personal qualities are respected but also because once one accepts their belief system then one just does not argue with the word of God, the final arbiter.

However, what characterises the members of many contemporary communes, particularly the young who are attracted to those of the self-actualising variety, is a desire to get away from any external authorities over their own lives and to create within the commune an environment where the individual can attain personal freedom and autonomy. Within such groups the attempts of particular members to assert their authority over the rest of the body can be an important source of conflict leading to the collapse of the venture. There is the danger that certain members will come to see themselves as the 'guru' of the commune, particularly if they were amongst those who originally founded the venture or contributed to the purchase of the property.

Religious communes of the past typically expected potential recruits to 'bear witness' to their conversion to the beliefs of the group and to their willingness to abide by its practices and standards. As such they at least ensured that the members of the group shared certain fundamental assumptions and beliefs in common. With many modern communes, however, little attention is paid to obtaining from potential members their assent to certain fundamental beliefs and to the commune's ways of going about things, as will be seen in the later chapters. The result can be that one finds a group of people living together who have little else in common than a desire to live in a commune. Consequently disagreements and conflict can emerge on a whole range of issues. These conflicts can occur over matters such as the general orientation of the commune—is it to be an 'outward looking' group, concerned with active involvement in the political affairs of the surrounding community, or is it going to be an 'inward looking' venture, with the emphasis upon the development of close, honest and open relationships between the members of the commune itself?

Conflict can occur over the sexual relationships between the members, and the position of women within the group. Thus one woman wrote feelingly of her experiences in communes in America:[18]

> The talk of love is profuse but the quality of relationships is otherwise. The hip man like his straight counterpart is nothing more, nothing less, than a predator. His sexual experience is largely an act of conquest or rape and certainly nothing more than an expression of hostility. The idea of sexual liberation for the woman means she is not so much free to fuck but free to get fucked over.

Conflict can occur through different attitudes towards the traditionally taken-for-granted role of the woman in the home as 'cook, dish-washer, child-minder and bed-warmer', particularly where the women of the commune seek liberation from the constraints of such roles and aspire to full equality with the other members as human beings rather than as women or men.

Very often the disagreements that lead to the eventual collapse of a communal venture are not so much over the matters of 'grand principle' which seem to cause the splitting-up of socialist groups, such as the question of whether the USSR is a degenerate workers' state or an example of state capitalism. Rather the tensions and grievance emerge out of differences concerning points of practical living, such as members holding to different standards of cleanliness, different attitudes towards child-rearing, different conceptions of what constitutes 'laziness', conflicting attitudes towards potential recruits, the use of drugs, and so on. One of the problems which is common to most communes, however, is that of privacy, or rather the lack of privacy. Thus, a writer on communal experiments in nineteenth-century America commented that[19]

> Some things the communist must surrender; and the most precious of these is solitude. The man to whom at intervals the faces and voices of his kind become hateful, whose bitterest need is sometimes to be alone—this man need not try communism.

Whilst for some continuous contact with fellow commune members is seen as an important means of developing self-awareness, for others such experiences cause great personal stress and inter-personal friction unless some allowance is made within the structure and organisation of the living experiment for them to get away from their fellow members from time to time. Most communes achieve this by providing a private room for each member.

Another problem encountered by members of communes which stems from the practice of group living and is related to the problem of privacy is that of the sacrifice of individual freedom that certain people feel is required of them within a commune. When one's life is led in the close company of others, then it follows that each individual's actions directly affect the lives of the other group members in some way or another. Whilst this is viewed by some as important in the development of a true spirit of brotherly love within the commune, others can experience it as a particularly tyrannical restriction upon their individual autonomy. This conflict between the twin ideas that inspire many ventures, the desire for individual freedom coupled with the desire for a close relationship with others, can also be made manifest over the issue of private property within the commune. Even where a group formally renounces the notion of private personal property, individual members can experience conflict between the desire to conform to the socialistic principles of the group and the concern to retain control, if not formal ownership, over what had previously been their own personal property. Thus, one commune member told me once of what he felt to be the personal hang-ups of living in a commune: 'for one brought up on "individualised" possessions—the feeling that one is not a completely free agent in spending money for such things as buying an amplifier or seeing friends in Scotland.' Another person, who was trying to form a commune, spoke of her worries about 'giving up a lot of personal possessions. I hate to think also that things we have had for a long time would be neglected by others, and that communal things would not be looked after by anybody.'

Of course, not all communes experience such problems. Certain groups do not practice communal possession of goods and property, whilst others take far greater account of their members' felt need for privacy than do others. Different groups experience different problems with varying degrees of intensity—this is one of the major themes to be explored in ensuing chapters. Likewise, different groups have different relationships with the 'outside world', according to such factors as their degree of apparent respectability and conventionality in matters of dress and life style, whether they use drugs or not, whether their group has been in existence for a short or a relatively long period of time, and so on.

However, radical secular and religious groups of the past that have sought to withdraw from the corrupt world to establish their own vision of the ideal society in miniature have traditionally come into conflict with the rest of society in general and with the representatives of the state in particular. Conflict has occurred in the past over the relationship of the individual to the state in such matters as the taking of oaths, attendance at state schools, the civil registration of marriage, compliance with public health regulations, conscription and the right of the individual to refuse to bear arms for the state. Such conflict is still experienced by communal groups, but in Britain at least, the major areas of confrontation between communes and the state appear to occur in the areas of police interference whilst searching for drugs, and the problems created by local authorities concerned about the compliance of the commune with public health regulations and the like.

Apart from conflict with the state, the hostility of the people inhabiting the area surrounding the living experiment was a problem which confronted many past communal ventures. Thus, the early attempt in the seventeenth century of the Diggers to create a co-operative colony in the south of England was frustrated by their neighbours who[20]

> set fire to six houses, and burned them down, and burned likewise some of their household stuff, and wearing clothes, throwing their beds, stools and household stuff, up and down the Common, not pitying the cries of many little children, and their frightened mothers, which are Parishioners born in the Parish.

Although certain groups in America would appear to have faced this kind of harassment, with people driving through the communal property firing off shot-guns at any stray signs of life they came across, this sort of practice does not appear to have been adopted by the neighbours of British communes, no matter what they might imagine goes on in their local outpost of the alternative society.[21] But again, the relationships that exist between the members of a commune and their surrounding neighbours vary according to the type of commune and change over time.

This question of how different types of commune change over time with regard to such things as their way of life and their relationships with their neighbours is the major concern of this book. What follows is an examination of five different ventures and how they have coped, in their different ways, with the problems of communal living. Two of them are located in Scotland, three in England. Two are urban-based, three are sited in rural areas. One has a membership of over 100, another has about 25 members, whilst the other three only have up to a dozen people in residence. Two are at least in part inspired by religious beliefs, the other three guided by beliefs drawn from other sources. Three of them have a membership which is mainly composed of young people, another is mainly inhabited by middle-aged folk, whilst a fifth has a membership made up of roughly equal proportions of young and older members.

In Chapter 2 the commune considered is an urban group in Edinburgh who came together in 1971 with the intention of establishing an urban base for their political activities. The commune examined in Chapter 3 is a rural venture in Norfolk which in many ways corresponds to the image that many people have of the hippie drop-out commune, and which differs from the activist commune of Edinburgh along many dimensions but particularly with regard to the over-all aim of the group, which could be classed as being of the self-actua-lising variety referred to above. The third group considered is a therapeutic commune in London which has as its aim the creation of a Christian community, an extended family, to care for those in need, the oppressed and the sick. As such it is an example of a commune which is inspired by religious beliefs but which has as its aim the secular goal of caring for those typically deemed 'socially inadequate' by the rest of society. A practical commune is the subject of Chapter 5—a group of people occupying a large hall in the Cots-wolds who were attracted to the idea of communal living largely by the promise of sharing living costs rather than by any grand idea for transforming society. The final experiment in communal living to be considered is the Centre of Light at Findhorn in the north of Scotland, which seeks to pioneer a new way of living through following God's guidance with the aim of bringing down the Kingdom of Heaven on Earth. This venture is inspired by a set of beliefs which display many of the characteristics of the mystic religions of the past, religious beliefs which contrast significantly with those which originally inspired the founders of the Kingsway Community which is the subject of Chapter 4. Through the examination of these five different ventures into the field of communal living it is hoped that readers will gain an insight into some of the alternatives to what one television broadcaster called 'the bra-encased bosom of the nuclear family' that are being created by increasing numbers of people, and thereby come to examine their own living arrangements with clearer eyes.

Chapter 2

Newhaven:
an activist commune
'A nice place to eat and sleep at.'

The distinguishing characteristic of activist communes is their orientation towards bringing about radical social change. The members of such groups typically seek to create the new social order and subvert the existing one not solely through the exemplary action of living together as a communal group but also through involving themselves in direct, radical political and social action at the 'grass-roots' level in the urban environment. Typically they believe in bringing about social change through people demanding an ever-increasing control of their own local environment, their neighbourhood and, in the process, their own lives. Generally their aim is the encouragement of participatory democracy within local communities, through encouraging local inhabitants to claim the right to decide and influence the decisions that affect their lives, rather than relying on the unseen 'powers-that-be-up-there' such as central and local government to make the decisions for them. Although the attitude of such groups differs from the orientation of the rural self-actualising communities with regard to their concern to involve themselves directly in the affairs of the world immediately outside their commune, they share certain positions in common. Amongst these, the most significant is their belief in the desirability and necessity for any movement for social change to be based on a grass-roots movement in which the decentralisation of decision-making is far-reaching, and of course they share a certain ground in so far as they choose to live in a communal fashion, sharing their lives with others.

It was because I was interested to see how such projects develop over time that I had written to a member of one such commune in Edinburgh asking if I could stay for a short while and outlining the nature of my interest in their venture in communal living. In an article written two years earlier when the commune was just starting, one of the members had said:[1]

The whole idea slowly crystallised among three or four people towards the end of last year (1970). A core of about seven quickly materialised, the common feature being a left-wing orientation. We had several meetings to discuss how we would organise the commune, most of the talk being about finance. Around February we started looking for a house. The idea at the time was to find a place in the sort of area that would give opportunities for political community work. . . .

The attitudes of the people in the group towards the idea of living communally are not all the same. Some people see it mainly as a functional base for a lot of people to live their own lives according to their different commitments, whereas others see it as being something for its own sake as well, an attempt at a different life style which tries to overcome some of the destructive effects of the capitalist system on *ourselves*—eg. private property instincts, individualism, cynicism, apathy, lack of creativity, lack of real communication with other people. I personally feel that while it is absolutely necessary to engage oneself in the class struggle, it is also necessary to develop in one's personal life the human values of socialism.

One of the problems that confronts groups of well-meaning radical young people who seek to plant themselves in the middle of a working-class estate and start generating radical activity amongst the local 'natives' is actually obtaining a physical base in such an area. Working-class areas are not exactly overflowing with property which will comfortably house up to a dozen people. This had been the problem that had faced other groups which I had known when I had lived in London. The problem was the same in that city which shares so many similarities with London ('a powdered face and a dirty arse'), Edinburgh. The Newhaven group had found it impossible to find a house suitable for their purposes in a working-class area. The house they eventually decided to occupy was a large three-storied villa, detached, in a middle-class residential area between Edinburgh and Leith, a few hundred yards from the southern shores of the Firth of Forth. The house itself was built around 1850 for a General Auchinleck who, rumour had it, had been a Governor-General of India. It is the kind of house which people from Liverpool would recognise in the Sefton Park area as once having belonged to someone who had made his money from the cotton trade. Like so many similar areas in other cities in Britain the houses were built for people when the styles of living led by the different classes were more overtly different. They are too big for modern middle-class families and they are being turned into flats and bed-sitters or taken over by charitable organisations as residential homes. Thus, next door to the commune was a Salvation Army house for 'fallen women', whilst the house on the other side had been bought by an ex-RAF officer who shared it with a number of lodgers.

Inside the house there were three floors. The ground floor had four large rooms which were used as a lounge and TV room and meeting place for the local group of International Socialists, the dining room, and the kitchen. On the first floor there were four bedrooms and a bathroom. The second floor had three bedrooms and yet another bathroom. The rooms themselves were very large and very tall. The house itself was pretty sparsely furnished.

The members themselves each had his own individual room. In contrast to the appearance of the 'long-haired-weirdo-freaks' who are typically to be found in the rural self-actualising communities, the members of the Newhaven community had the fairly conventional appearance of slightly 'turned-on' students. The men had collar length hair rather than shoulder length, they didn't wear beads and bangles, and they wore shoes. The difference between the women in Newhaven and those I had met in the rural communes was epitomised for me when I discovered that the girl in whose room I was sleeping had left behind her vaginal deodorant spray.

Origins and recruitment of members

The origins and initial aims of the Newhaven commune resembled very closely those of an urban communal group that was living in south London when I had contacted them two years previously. This similarity was not totally due to coincidence. One of the members of the London group had moved up to Edinburgh for a year to study. He had talked of the English commune and the ideas behind it with the people he met whilst in the North. These people were mainly students and members of the Student Christian Movement. The political position of the members of the founder group in Edinburgh was described to me by one of their number as involving a 'radical Christian stance' towards political and social issues. By this she meant that they had all shared a moralistic revulsion against many aspects of life in our capitalist society and a commitment to seek to do something about such conditions, but that they lacked any total, all-embracing and coherent view of the situation which would enable them to fit individual and apparently isolated phenomena into the context of a general explanatory framework—that is, they were not 'scientific socialists' in those days.

Like the members of the London commune, the members of the Edinburgh group had come together as students, and since leaving university, whilst living in the commune, they had pursued their post-graduate careers. Thus, one member worked as an architect, another was doing a PhD, another was a teacher, another member was a social worker, whilst an American member was studying Divinity at Edinburgh University. One of the permanent members, another social worker, was away staying with her boyfriend during my visit. These were the six permanent members, but there were also half a dozen more people living in the house during my stay who were not permanent members.

The original group had all come together as friends, students, members of the Student Christian Movement and of a radical orientation. Of the original eleven, however, there had been quite a turn-over of members. Seven of the original group had left, leaving only five of the founder members still living there. Why this fairly rapid turnover? In the first place the members of such communes are frequently people who are also pursuing a professional career of one sort or another. They are not people who believe in 'dropping out' into the rural wastes. As a result Newhaven has suffered from people having to move in search of employment and professional advancement. Thus one of the earliest to leave was one who finished his course at the university and took up a post in the South. Other people had left because they felt that the commune was not the place for them although they have remained in Edinburgh and remain in close contact with the commune members.

Discussing the reasons why people left, one member felt that one

couple did so because they did not fit into the group largely because
they were from different social origins from the rest of the members.
The bulk of the members have come from middle-class family backgrounds. This couple were from working-class families, although the
girl had been to university. Despite their political beliefs, the middle-
class members were offended by the ways of the working-class
couple—their public arguing and fighting, the way the girl stubbed
her cigarettes out in the bread crusts left on the breakfast plates, the
way she borrowed people's clothes and forgot to return them and
so on. Eventually the couple left but have kept close contact with
the group and were staying there temporarily during my visit.
Another member talked of the couples that had left, pointing out
that communes did not seem to fit couples. Thus, one of the original
members was in the process of finding a flat for himself and his newly-
married wife because they wanted to set up a place of their own,
away from the commune which the girl disliked and felt threatened
by. In a letter to me one of the members talked of the people who
were leaving the commune for one reason or another:

> There have been quite a few changes over the summer, and for
> one reason or another four people are likely to be moving out—
> one was only here for a year anyway, two blokes have formed
> relationships during the year and their girlfriends—in one case,
> wife—don't want to live in the commune, so both are moving
> out to live in flats. One bloke can't stand his job and has
> chucked it and is planning on going to Italy with his girlfriend
> and so has moved out to save money—although he was one of
> the best and most enthusiastic members of the house.

Another of the female members was planning to leave. Her boyfriend was heavily into the use of hallucinogenic drugs and as the
only formal rule of the house was that no dope was allowed on the
property for fear of a police bust, the commune was obviously not
the place for them. Another of the girlfriends of one of the male
members was described as a lovely girl who was very shy and who
felt very threatened by all the people living at the house—she and
her boyfriend had moved into a flat by the time of my visit. Again,
one couple who had formed the nucleus of the original group had
separated and the husband had moved out into a neighbouring
flat. During the year they were together as members of the commune
he had been working 120 hours a week as a houseman in a local

c

hospital. On the only day off he could enjoy, the house would be full of people with whom he felt he could not relate, shattered as he was by his work—again he felt threatened by the other members.

People have of course come along to replace those that have left. New members arrive mainly as friends of people who are already living there, or they get to know about the place through friends and visitors to the commune. There is no formal procedure for admission—there are just some people who spend some time at the commune and naturally seem to fit in with the group. Whilst there is no questioning of any prospective member's political beliefs in order to assess specifically their suitability for membership of the group, all members tended to be fairly radical in their beliefs—as one member put it, 'obviously no roaring right winger would want to come here anyway'. Although, when asked, no member could imagine a situation arising where they would formally agree that 'such and such types of person are not eligible for membership here as opposed to such and such other types', at the same time, in exercising their judgement as to whether anyone who was interested in joining the group would 'fit in' or not, certain criteria apart from political orientation played their part. One of these was age—all the members are in their twenties. Another was whether the person appeared to be sufficiently stable in his or her emotional and mental development. Thus, some weeks prior to my visit the group had held one of its infrequent and relatively rare house meetings to discuss the situation of the house with regard to future membership resulting from the present turnover of members. One of the people they considered as someone who might want to join them was aged 45. He had been recently divorced after years of marriage. After a life spent farming he had moved to Edinburgh to train as a social worker where he had established contact with the group. In explaining their hesitation to come to a decision about this person, one of the members expressed it as follows:

> 'We're not sure about him as there is such a difference in age and it would mean such a great change for him in his way of life. Also there is an element of desperation about it on his part and we are not sure whether we are sufficiently mature and stable to take this.'

Relations with outside

As a commune which had as one of its original aims that of acting
as some sort of 'red base' within an urban area which would be
involved in helping to develop campaigns and programmes oriented
towards affairs of concern to the local inhabitants, it might have
been expected that the commune would have close links with the
people who lived in that area. In fact, as has been remarked, they
failed to obtain suitable property in a working-class area as they
had originally hoped to do. This had obviously influenced their
plans as an activist commune, which involved establishing close
links with the local populus. These initial plans had also undergone
a transformation as a result of another unforseen development.
Simply stated, this development was that amongst the original
members who did consider themselves as political activists there
had been a change in political beliefs. Of the five original members
who were still members of the commune, four had become members
of the International Socialists and had adopted the policies and
strategies of that political organisation with regard to how to
engineer a socialist revolution. No longer did they believe in going
into a working class area from the 'outside', so to speak, in so far as
they were all middle class students and professionals. Their policy
now was to work within the organisations, professional associations,
and trade unions of which they were members, trying to promote a
socialist consciousness and socialist policies amongst their fellow
members at the grass-roots level. As a consequence, they were no
longer interested in trying to talk with and convert their immediate
neighbours. They made no attempt to proselytise their beliefs
through personal contacts with the occupants of the surrounding
houses, but rather *as individuals* concentrated their political
activities on those organisations of which they, as individuals, were
members. This in fact was the self-same pattern as was revealed by
the commune in London with whom they had had some links.

Whilst they, as a commune, were no longer too concerned about
turning their neighbours on to their way of life and way of viewing
things, this is not to say that their neighbours took no interest in the
commune's activities and existence. As I found with many other
communes, whether rural or urban based, the most positive attitudes
towards the group had been displayed by the local clergy. Thus, they
had heard that a local clergyman in his sermon one Sunday had

started talking about 'the group of young people who are trying to live a new and alternative way of life'. Others in the neighbourhood had not shown such tolerance, however. The members believed that many of their local neighbours thought that the house was some sort of hippie dwelling place, a scene of orgies and drug abuse—a completely erroneous belief. This attitude did not worry or bother the members in any way. They laughed when they told me of the time they awoke one morning to find the word 'brothel' daubed over their front door. Although the commune as such had few links with their neighbours, as individuals they naturally had some contact of one form or another. One of the members, an American Divinity student who was completely apolitical, in the sense that he claimed he had no time for politicians or for any of the members of IS as political actors, had a long-standing aim of establishing a farm in Nova Scotia, Canada, where orphans could go and live and work the land. He loved children and had made friends with a number of local kids who would call round at weekends to play in the garden and help him tend the small vegetable plot which he was trying to cultivate.

Although the commune members as a group were not overly concerned about what their neighbours thought of them, they were worried about the possibility of interference and harrassment from the police. In fact they had suffered no harrassment whatsoever from the police. As individuals, some of their number had been arrested on various demonstrations in Edinburgh. However, they feared being bust by the police. As a result they made it a strict rule of the house that no drugs were to be allowed on the premises.

Just as the members did not participate as a group in any political group or organisation but solely as individual members of such organisations, so the commune itself did not possess any formal links with any other communes, or the Commune Movement itself. In fact, they seemed reluctant to talk of themselves as a commune, and in conversation one found oneself talking about the 'house' or the 'group' rather than the 'commune'. In part this reluctance to broadcast themselves as a commune stemmed from the felt lack of sympathy displayed for rural communes by those members who were active in local IS groups—they talked disparagingly about those people who 'sit around on their arses all day in the country thinking that through changing themselves they are going to change the world'. For them the revolutionary hope for the future lay with the working class rising up against the capitalist class guided by the correct leadership. Significant change would only take place in the factories at the point of production, not out in the countryside. Apart from such theoretical antagonisms towards the rural commune dwellers, many of them also felt that they would go insane living an isolated existence in the countryside away from the urban centres. It was largely due to this lack of sympathy with the philosophy held and the life styles led by their stereotyped image of the rural 'drop-out' that they had consciously avoided any publicity about their venture in any of the underground literature or in *Communes* magazine. They had a strong fear of being over-run by long-haired drug freaks if their existence became generally known around the underground circuit.

Likewise, as individuals, their outside contacts were with the more traditional forms of radical organisation such as the International Socialists, the trade unions and so on, rather than with newer forms such as free schools and the like, with their emphasis upon developing alternative structures to replace existing institutions rather than confronting the existing ones in a head-on confrontation.

What had happened with this group was that their definition of the commune had changed over time, and this changed definition had the consequences for the life and activities of its members which I have been describing. Partly due to the fact that when the commune was founded different members had different ideas of what they wanted to achieve within the commune, and partly because a number of the driving forces within the original group had changed their political ideas and positions, their attitude toward the commune had changed. It had changed from one where the project was important and significant as a commune in itself to one where their attitude towards the commune was little more than that it was a nice place to live and eat and sleep, a useful kind of roof over the individual's head amidst nice company while they got on with the more important tasks as individuals of involving themselves with promoting the cause of international socialism around Edinburgh. Thus, since they did not consider their commune itself, as a way of life, very significant as a revolutionary means of changing society, they did not attempt to proselytise and convert others to their way of life. They did not produce any literature of their own such as other communal groups have done. The literature that was sold by the members of the commune was mainly the *Socialist Worker*, the paper of the International Socialists.

Internal organisation

This attitude towards the commune was reflected in its organisation. Apart from the rule about no drugs on the premises, the only other sign of any formalised routines for coping with the business of living together as a group was a piece of paper attached to the kitchen door on which people wrote down their names according to which days they would or could make the evening meal or do the washing up. Two people were responsible each day for making the evening meal for the purposes of which they drew out of the communal purse the sum of £1·50. Two people also took responsibility for washing up. It was left up to individuals to fill in their names on the rosta, no one person took responsibility for filling the blank spaces with names. There was no division of labour on sexual grounds whatsoever. In similar manner it was left up to the individual members themselves to take responsibility for cleaning up particular areas of the house such as the hallway, the stairs, the dining area and so on. This was how it was meant to be. In practice people did not clean the house at regular periods, rather someone would get fed up with, say, the state of the hallway and set about cleaning it up. The only other sign of a division of labour was the post of treasurer which one person held until he was fed up with the task when it would pass on to someone else. In addition, Bobby, the American student, took it upon himself to develop a small vegetable patch in the back garden, an interest which none of the other members shared.

They did not have regular decision-making house meetings. This was partly because of the nature of the membership. It proved very difficult to get everyone together at one time as so many of the members were out and about involved in their own personal lives in the city. During the week people were out at work or studying or visiting friends in the evening, whilst at weekends people were out selling newspapers, attending meetings or enjoying themselves in the city. As a result they relied heavily upon a small blackboard in the dining room as a means of communicating messages and information to each other. They did all meet together over the evening meal which was a communal event but it was rare that the members gathered together specifically to discuss the affairs of the commune. As was remarked above, I was informed that a meeting had been held a few weeks prior to my visit but this reflected the state of flux that the commune had been experiencing during that period, with people leaving and the remaining members feeling the need to discuss questions concerning new members. Just as the commune did not have any regular system of house meetings to decide issues, they did not have any regular meetings at which an attempt was made to bring out the grievances felt by individual members and to relieve the tensions that do build up between members. That they did not have any regular decision-making meetings reflected the fact that for most of the members the commune represented little more than a nice place to sleep and eat, and as such it was felt that there were no common issues upon which a decision needed to be reached. From this perspective, any meeting that was held was, by definition, an extra-ordinary meeting. Likewise, the fact that the members did not concern themselves with meeting together to try and relieve tensions and develop more open and honest relationships with each other reflected their almost complete lack of concern with this aspect of communal living, an aspect which reigns paramount in the minds of many young people who have joined rural groups as part of a search for self-fulfilment, self-discovery and at the same time a sense of brotherhood with others. The concern of most of the members was with outside activities, whether this was work or their political activities. As such they felt that they had little time for the kind of deep, introspective analysis of themselves and of their relationships with the other members of the community that is a characteristic of many of the self-actualising communes.

The only kind of group activity that the members seemed to involve themselves in was the evening meal, and occasionally they would all go off into the Scottish highlands for a day's fell-walking. One of the members told me that they used to have a group reading after the evening meal when one of the members would read aloud to the others from some book or other. Trotsky and Wilhelm Reich were two of the authors that he mentioned. However, this practice had ceased with the coming of spring as people began to increase their involvement in outside activities and so the times when everyone was gathered together for the evening meal became rarer. Another member mentioned that this practice disappeared at least partly because it was never properly organised.

In a rural commune there is frequently little apparent difference between the organisation of life during the week and the daily routine that is apparent at weekends. In an urban commune such as that at

Newhaven where all the members were employed in work outside the commune, the difference between a weekday and a Saturday or Sunday was quite marked. During the week people got up, got themselves some breakfast and went out to work. The house was then emptied of occupants except for those who were not working for some reason and those who were visiting the group—friends, and political colleagues from out of town, who were temporarily excused the necessity to turn out to earn their daily bread. The house slowly filled up again towards evening as people returned from work or from their studies. The evening meal took place round about seven o'clock and when it was finished people then went off to do whatever was on their personal agenda for that evening. This might involve going to their own rooms to study, or read or listen to records. It might simply involve just moving into the lounge to watch television and talk, or an evening out selling papers or attending political meetings. Occasionally the lounge was occupied by a meeting of the local members of the International Socialists. At weekends the house had the appearance of any house occupied by young people on their days off from work. People got up when they felt like it, helped themselves to breakfast and then went about their individual affairs until it was time for the evening meal. It was rare that people were all gathered together as a group except for the evening meal. This was usually a substantial two-course meal followed by coffee. The commune purchased as many things as possible in bulk from a local 'cash'n' carry'.

Finance

As remarked above, the meal itself, like all groceries was purchased out of the common purse. Each member contributed the whole of his or her income into the common pool, and it was out of this that all the commune's bills were paid, by whoever happened to be treasurer at that time. In addition each person was allowed £4·50 a week for his personal expenditure. However, if a person had to pay a membership fee for, say, some professional organisation, in order for him to retain employment, then the commune would pay the necessary sum. The £4·50 was expected to pay for bus fares, cigarettes, and so on. In addition to this weekly amount each person could draw £50 a year out of the holiday fund that the commune had established, again financed by the contributions of the members. Other funds financed out of these contributions included an amount set aside in order to pay for any repairs that became necessary for the house. A political fund had also been established out of which any fines or expenses incurred by members through involvement in political activities could be paid. The mortgage and loan repayments incurred through the purchase of the property were also paid out of the communal purse.

The house itself was purchased in 1971 for a price of £13,000. The deposit was raised by people putting money together, but largely by one couple who sold their flat and put what money they had left, after repaying their building society loan, towards the deposit. The mortgage itself was obtained by this same couple, but due to the age of the property they obtained only an 80 per cent loan. By late 1972 they still owed the people who sold them the property something like £500 as they could not raise the full £13,000 at the time of purchase. Mortgage and loan repayments amounted to about £140 a month. They had no rule about the financial contribution made by people when they joined, although members I talked with on this matter seemed to think that when a person joined the commune, they would be expected to contribute their assets into the common pool, but whether this would actually be the case or not would depend on the situation. Thus, one of the existing members had a couple of hundred pounds in the bank, but as she feared a demand for this amount of money from the Irish government (she was from Eire) everyone considered it perfectly reasonable that she should keep this money for herself in case of the feared eventuality.

The lives of communes of the past have been torn by strife for many reasons. One source of dissent has stemmed from the financial problems arising when a member who has made a significant financial contribution to the community has demanded repayment on his departure. Fortunately for the group at Newhaven this situation had not arisen. Those who had left had not made any great financial contribution towards the deposit necessary to buy the place. One member who had left was the husband of one of the remaining members, and it had been this couple who had raised most of the deposit and in whose name the mortgage had been raised. He had moved into a small flat in the neighbourhood and the commune had lent him £300 to enable him to purchase the property. It was antici-pated by the remaining members that when the time came for a per-son to leave who had made a significant contribution in financial terms to the commune, then each case would be decided upon individually. Thus, if the commune had a lot of money available, then people might be given or lent some of it—but this would be an *ad hoc* decision made for each individual case. It was also vaguely anticipated that if the commune ever ceased to exist, then the house would probably be sold and if any profit was made on the transaction then this might well be donated to some revolutionary organisation such as FRELIMO.

What these financial arrangements of the commune illustrated was the commitment felt by the members to the socialist ideals which many of them held. When asked why they pooled all their income, one member replied in the following terms: 'Each one of us is doing his work, and although we do different things, each person's work is as valid as the next person's, so that's why we pool our different levels of income and each takes out equal amounts for his personal expenditure.' Despite this approach, however, each member retained control over his own personal possessions such as clothes, records and such like.

Problems and future prospects

Although the socialist principles adhered to by the original members revealed themselves in such things as the financial arrangements, by the autumn of 1972, after eighteen months' existence, the commune as a group adhered to no single coherent belief system. Those who had worked out a 'political position' did not consider the commune as particularly significant in their anticipated scheme for social change—a working-class revolution. As such, their attitude towards the commune was that it was little more than a very pleasant house in which to live and sleep, and a useful place to live in so far as there one could find people who shared one's beliefs and with whom one could share the chores of daily existence, thereby obtaining more free time to spend on one's political activities. The commune itself as a group of people living together was not particularly important in itself, other than that they were good company. But, given the subordinate position occupied by the commune in the scheme of things as perceived by those who did have clear ideas about the existing social order and how to change it, then the commune itself avoided many of the problems that have plagued other groups. Thus, they had no problems stemming from conflict over group policy and group goals, as they did not think of themselves as a unified body who could be expected to agree upon such things. They were individuals living in the commune involved with their own lives which happened to cross and mix with the lives of the other members in various ways, but the life of the commune was made up of these separate threads rather than constituting a single coherent 'group life'. As individuals, members might have their own life goals and revolutionary aspirations, but for the commune they had no other goal but that it should remain a nice place to live. Since they all agreed upon this issue, the division of the group over questions of principle, group policy and communal goals did not arise.

The major problems referred to by members in discussion related primarily to three areas: the problem of couples, the problem of getting on with difficult members, and the problem of housework. As mentioned above, a number of those who had left the commune had been couples. It would seem that an important source of membership loss for urban communes can occur when a member meets someone with whom h⌐ or she wishes to live and that person is from outside the commune, has no experience of communal living, and has little genuine desire to sample the life. The commune itself must appear as something of a threat to the stranger—all those people who have lived with and shared the life of the man or woman you want for yourself. It would seem perfectly natural for the outsider to feel the commune as a threat to his or her relationship with the other, and to avoid this by persuading the other to leave the group. In fact, within the Newhaven commune, each member of any couple had his own individual room. This was partly due to the belief of the members that they should develop as individuals rather than as couples dependent upon each other.

Other problems facing the members of the commune included the usual ones of how to cope with members who were 'difficult' in the sense that they tended to bring the other members down or just simply were not very popular with the other members. At New-haven, as has been remarked, people coped with this problem by avoiding it rather than confronting it. They had a middle-class fear of appearing to be 'rude' to people. They had tried to be 'kind' in their relationships with each other, and so would find it very difficult to proclaim openly their dislike for a particular charac-teristic of an individual member in an attempt to 'clear the air' and establish more open and honest relationships with each other. Thus.

when I arrived at the house on one occasion with a member, we entered the hallway to find it being scrubbed and washed down by a grim-faced female member. An attempted friendly word was met with a grunt and a murmur and continued scrubbing and cleaning activity. 'That's just Lisa doing her moral bit,' it was explained to me. 'You get used to it. We just take it with a pinch of salt.'

Lisa had expressed interest in joining the group when she first heard of their plans through the Student Christian Movement. She had been living and teaching in Liverpool and contact was lost with her. The next the group heard was that she had taken a job in Edinburgh to enable her to join the commune. Unfortunately they had no room available by that time. This caused Lisa herself to believe that the commune did not want her as a member, and this feeling of occasional antagonism and bitterness against the other members had remained since she had become a member. In talking with the members one got the impression that they had thought long and hard about admitting her to the group but in the end felt obliged to have her as she herself had assumed she was to be among the original members. The most obvious difference between her and the other members was that she was far more withdrawn into herself. She seemed to find it particularly difficult to relate to other people. However, none of this was discussed by all the members together in an attempt to improve the atmosphere, and so it simmered on just below the surface only to emerge when she did her 'moral bit'.

Other problems arose through people having different standards of cleanliness and tidiness, through people forgetting to clean up those areas of the house that they had agreed to, and other such occurrences. What happened in such situations was that the housework tended to fall on one or two members who either had higher standards of tidiness than the others, had more free time, or enjoyed cleaning and tidying.

The future

Given the failure in terms of longevity of life displayed by many of the non-religious communal groups of the past, what about the future of the Newhaven commune? One would anticipate that it will continue to experience a turnover of members as those who have embarked upon professional careers are required to move out of the region in pursuit of employment. As more members find people with whom they wish to live, so one would expect others to leave to set up home for themselves. The members themselves had no plans for the commune as such. They did not anticipate developing commune-based industries or whatever. They did think about keeping the house in repair and they did express a wish that it should continue to house a commune for as long as possible, even after all the present members had left. If this did not happen for some reason, then it was anticipated, as has been remarked, that the house would be sold and the profits donated to some worthy revolutionary of humanitarian cause. Of course it could happen that new members might arrive who would seek to change the direction of the commune, who would try to make the venture into a far more self-conscious kind of thing with plans and schemes for the development of the commune and the people in it as something worthwhile in itself. If such a situation did arise, then one would expect a real conflict situation to emerge within the commune. Once someone has been introduced to socialism, has started to read Marx and Lenin and believes that here he has the *truth*— scientific socialism no less—then they become very intolerant and scathing about those with whom they do not agree, particularly 'bourgeois romantics' who are interested in communal living for its own sake and for the sake of increasing their self-awareness. Thus, one would expect that the International Socialists amongst the members of the commune would exercise their veto power on potential members who strongly expressed a desire to change the commune's way of operating.

However, it was just this concern with developing their self-awareness that characterised the members of the self-actualising, rural-based commune in Norfolk which I visited after taking my leave of Newhaven.

Chapter 3

Shrubb Family:
a self-actualising commune

'We dig living together, and it's as simple as that.'

I drove through the Norfolk countryside in beautiful sunshine and without too much difficulty found the unmade track leading up to the cottages which house the Shrubb Family. Originally a seventeenth-century farmhouse which had been divided into cottages some time later, the buildings are sited in about an acre of land bounded on three sides by the fields of their local farmer and by the track on the east side. When I visited the commune in 1970 the property consisted of some twenty-odd small rooms, although the members were living in the north cottage which had electricity and a water supply whilst they busied themselves renovating the rest of the building. The garden and land in front of the cottages in 1970 resembled a cross between a builder's yard and an overgrown area of waste land. So, the first change I noticed on my arrival in 1972 was the apparent improvement in the gardens at the front, bounded as it was by a multi-coloured fence adorned with banners flying from tall poles.

I was met with a friendly wave by Nicholas and his brother-in-law, a long-term visitor, who were passing timber through a window as a fuel supply for the winter fire in the house. The passage of time had also seen a great change in the interior. To the left of the front door was the south cottage which they were in the process of renovating. They were planning to convert it into a second lounge to increase the communal relaxation space. To the right of the front door was the main living area consisting of the dining area dominated by the old Aga solid fuel stove. Through this area on a slightly lower level was the lounge with a large old-fashioned fireplace built into the north wall. A scullery, wash-room, pantry, and a bedroom were also located on the ground floor whilst upstairs were the bedrooms and, looking slightly out of place amongst the sloping floors, old timbers, and plaster was the new bathroom, wood lined with a modern bath and bog which was installed with the aid of a house improvement grant from the local authority. The major structural alterations that had taken place since my first visit consisted largely of walls having been demolished to make larger rooms whilst electricity had also been installed throughout the house by one of the ex-members.

Origins and beliefs

The commune had its origin in 1970 when the founder inherited a couple of thousand pounds and bought the property after having seen it empty and enquiring in the neighbourhood about the possibility of purchase. Although the commune originally consisted of four members, this number was increased up to about a dozen in the first year of existence by visitors and friends coming to stay for various periods of time. The original four members were all friends who had lived together in London. One of their number wrote of the over-all goal or purpose that underpinned their venture in communal living:

> We want to develop this place not simply as a retreat for people all of the same age and type, but a place where people of all ages and outlooks can come and live our way of life with us. Also we would like to feel part of the local community and have them see what we are doing and accept us.

They had also told me of their aim of creating 'that environment where all that is possible can be possible . . . to become self-sufficient; a happy and beautiful place to live; to be artistic and have a valuable artistic output and help others to see the light.' As such, the commune appeared as a perfect example of those self-actualising communes whose members seek to create the environment in which they can discover their true selves and develop their creative potentialities within the context of a commune, and in the process seek to create a new alternative social order.

In pursuit of their conception of the proper life such people have been led to drop out of the straight society, but this opting out is viewed not merely as a negative turning of one's back upon the old

society. Rather, there is the belief that the only way to change the
social order is through living one's own life according to one's values
of individual freedom and the non-exploitation of one's fellow men
and nature, and through the power of example cause others to
question the *status quo* and their individual life within it, thereby
hastening the creation of an alternative society. As one of the early
members of the commune expressed it to me soon after the formation of the venture:

> 'By living our own lives here we can develop a kind of seed that
> can grow while the old is dying around it. In this way the new
> will develop out of the old, as people withdraw their support from
> the old. It's a question of awareness—of gradually trying to make
> others more aware so that others develop some thoughts about
> us. In doing this they may begin to think in new ways. Even if it
> doesn't change them, it may change others with whom they
> talk. . . . By living in communes and by living a different way of
> life we can make some people sit up and think—"maybe there is
> another way of life, maybe we ought to change our way of life." '

There was the feeling amongst the founder members that they were
involved in the creation of 'the germ of a new society within the
old'. A new society, as one of the original members described it to
me,

> 'which is based on a very different system of values and norms
> which are, in a sense, socialist—in the sense of anti-capitalist—
> but at the same time not political. It is basing economic action
> and such on different sorts of motives than profit and money. It
> is because of other people that you do something and not out of
> the profit that you are going to get out of it.'

By 1972, although none of the orginal members of the community
remained, the general principles that had guided the initial foundation of the venture were still adhered to by the members. All of them
shared a disgust with 'straight society'. Just as one of the original
members mentioned that one of the prime personal advantages of
living in the commune was 'People—being able to turn to someone',
so one of the 1972 members replied to my question of what was the
attraction of living there—'We dig living together, and it's as simple
as that.' Again, just as with the original members there was a concern to live to an extent 'outside the system' according to their

values, in the hopes of turning others on through their example, so
the present members were inspired by a belief that one must live
one's life now according to one's beliefs, thereby hoping to change
people and society, rather than merely employing oneself in political
agitation of one sort of another for an hour a week and then going
back to living a conventional life and in the process supporting the
very economic, political and social systems that one opposes. Such
an attitude contrasts sharply with the orientation of the Newhaven
commune.

Thus, they saw it as important that they were open to visitors in
order that they, the visitors, could gain experience of alternative
forms of living and relating to people. One member recounted one
of their successes in this direction—the local fish and chip shop
owner had changed to using vegetable oil for frying at least partly
because he was aware of the fact that the members of the commune
were all vegetarians. Perhaps this change was directed solely by a
concern for their custom, but it was viewed as a small success for the
commune by its members. However, they did not believe in proselytising—according to their way of thinking there is no one single way
of living one's life. It was sufficient that they lived their life, that
others saw them living this life, and then made up their own minds
and drew their own conclusions about things. As such, they remained
true to the essentially non-coercive, anarcho-pacifist conception of
social change adhered to by the original members, one of whom
talked to me on my first visit of his thoughts about the part communes might play in the process of social change:

'I think they can influence ideas and I think by the very fact that
there are hundreds and thousands of people living in communes
and are living a different way of life, they can make some people
sit up and think "maybe there is another way of life, maybe we
ought to change our way of life". For one thing, communes are
not setting out to exert some sort of influence, they are not
preaching—they have changed things for themselves and that is
enough, if people want to follow, fair enough.'

Allied with this concern with 'turning others on' there was amongst
the members in 1972 a concern with individual self-development,
with increasing self-awareness that was also displayed by the original
members, whether this concern be expressed in spiritual terms or
not. All the members agreed that communal living was a much

D

richer life than that allowed within the confines of the nuclear family. As one member expressed it:

> 'Living here is a religious thing—not in the mystical but in a practical sense. Outside you might try and get people to do things the way you want them to do them. Here nobody will take any notice so you have to examine yourself to work out whether such things are really important or not.'

Another talked of how there was a 'spiritual thing' about living in the commune which was difficult to describe but involved a spiritual development through living together and close to the land.

Certainly what struck me about the commune, apart from the changes in the physical structure, was how little had changed over the two years in terms of the belief system adhered to by the members. Their own verdict was similar. As one member put it: 'The place has not changed in its direction, but it has become better. The people here now are very much into living with each other. Those into other things, like monogamous couples, have left.' As this remark implies, the degree to which any group retains its commitment to its original ideals and aims depends, amongst other things, upon the personnel who become involved in the group, whether the people who replace departed members share the original commitment or not. Therefore it seems relevant to examine the ways in which people have arrived to live at the commune and also the processes by which others have left.

Recruitment

> A new commune has started in Norfolk. Out of the talking and planning has at last come something concrete. We started talking about the idea of forming a commune sometime last summer. There were three of us, Ian, twenty, who had just chucked university after one year of an English degree, Anne, eighteen, who had just left school and Owen, twenty one, who had also left university after doing one year's sociology. Later a fourth person, Frankie, who is seventeen, joined us.

This was the original nucleus of the commune as described by one of their number in 1970.[1] However, during the early period numbers fluctuated. Two of the original members left early on and the remaining couple were joined by another pair—an ex-graduate and his American girl-friend. These four were in turn joined by another university drop-out from England who had been inspired with the idea of communal living after having travelled around some communes in America. By August 1970 it was estimated by one of the members that they had had up to fifty people staying with them at one time or another during the previous five months. During this early period they had no rules about who could or could not join them. They estimated that they would eventually expand to about eight or ten permanent members but in the meantime they felt very strongly that anyone who did join them should be a friend above all else, and a communard second. That is, they placed far greater importance on personal compatibility as a criterion for membership than upon any formally articulated belief or philosophy adhered to by the prospective member. Therefore it was expected of anyone who sought to join them that they would visit in the first instance, spend some time at the commune, and then commit themselves to living there by mutual agreement.

This absence of any formalised structure or process of recruitment continued to characterise the procedures of the commune in 1972, despite the fact that none of the original members remained. The practice as it existed after two years was for people to visit and stay at the commune for a while. During this period, if the person got on well with the other members and they with him or her, then it might occur to the visitor that the commune would be a nice place to live for a longer period of time. The prospective member would then probably raise the possibility with one of the existing members, who would give him his own personal opinion as to the likely response of the other members. If encouraged by this response or if the two decided that the matter should be raised with all the members, a discussion would take place amongst all the members with the prospective member present, over a meal or, if all the members happened to be gathered together, in the kitchen. If all the members welcomed the addition to their ranks, then the prospective member would be accepted. If there was any disagreement then the 'applicant' would be turned down—each member possessing, for want of a better phrase, a 'veto power' over any applications for membership.

Of course people did not arrive at the commune completely out of the blue. There are certain well-defined paths that are typically trodden by those who seek to become members of communes. Not only must people become disenchanted with the straight world as it appears to them, and with their own way of life within that world, they must also come to be aware of the existence of communes in general as places where 'people like them', people with whom they can identify, seek to live out a more rewarding kind of life. Furthermore they must also learn of the existence of particular communes such as the one in Norfolk before they can ever seek to become a member. Each individual member of any commune will have travelled a different path on the way to becoming a communard, but each one will have passed through these stages.

Thus, Dave, an Australian member of the commune, left school at 16 because he was fed up with it. He wanted to work with his hands rather than do clerical work, so he became apprenticed as a fitter and turner. He had a few friends who were art students with whom he spent his leisure time. He spent more and more of his spare time with these friends, he started to use dope, and before long he had packed in his job and was on the road to England. As he explained it:

> 'It's all to do with changing social groups. You start to grow your hair long. You start to smoke dope and you fit in more with them. You find people you really dig and you just don't fit in with the old lot anymore.'

He stayed with his brother in England, but began thinking about living in a commune. He was fed up with working for someone else from nine 'til five each day. Also, he was influenced by what he saw of the ways other people lived when he was travelling in Asia, the way such people lived co-operatively, sharing their food and their possessions with each other. Also, whilst he was on the road he had met many people who told him of communes. Having seen the magazine *Communes* and having read of the commune in Norfolk he wrote to it asking about joining. He also wrote to other communes. Three months after writing he received a reply inviting him to come and visit. He came and stayed. Dave, by the autumn of 1972, had been at the commune for two years. During this time he had received a small inheritance so he had returned to Australia to sample the life over there again. It was not to his liking and after being away for a few months he returned to Norfolk.

Sid, the oldest member who was in his thirties, had followed a different path to the commune but had passed through similar stages. He had been an engineer in the Merchant Navy for twelve years. Whilst travelling around the world he had started to smoke dope and started to mix in 'head' circles. He became interested in Buddhism. Dissatisfied with his life at sea he and a few friends began to talk about forming a commune. They all dropped out of the scheme eventually. He himself felt that he wanted to do something more than just smoke dope and whilst on leave he came across *Communes* magazine. He wrote to the secretary of the Commune Movement who gave him the address of the commune in Norfolk. He arrived in the summer of 1971 and stayed for four months on an extended leave. He then went back to sea for five months while he worked his notice and returned to the commune for Christmas 1971 where he has stayed ever since.

Jake had, like many other members of similar communes, dropped out of university before completing his course. After a period at home he set off to travel, armed with a copy of *Uncareers: a Directory of Alternative Work*.[2] A friend at university had been involved in organising work forces to visit communes in Britain to carry out construction work and other tasks. Thus, in the summer of 1971 Jake had spent a week as a member of one of these work forces at the commune in Norfolk. Having set out to travel round the country he had been in the neighbourhood of the commune in the early summer of 1972. He called in and stayed for a fortnight helping with the renovation work that has so far been a permanent characteristic of life at the commune. After two weeks he came to the decision that it would be a rewarding environment in which to live. He was accepted by the others as a member.

Nicholas and his wife had lived in the commune for over a year. He had left school at 15 and had started working as a labourer on building sites around the country. Eventually he became tired of this life and decided to attend classes to study for his 'A' Levels. He passed his examinations and went to university to study Philosophy. He left college after a term and with his wife and young child he began travelling round the country fruit-picking and doing odd jobs. With winter coming on after the fruit-picking season, however, they had no money and nowhere to stay. They moved to Norfolk to find out about renting cottages for the winter and whilst in Norfolk they discovered the commune.

Val and Ernest had been married for five years and had beer

living in London with their three children. Tired of the constraints
and pressures that a nuclear family life created and desiring to live a
life more closely aligned with their beliefs than was possible in
straight society, they contacted the Commune Movement and
began to travel round a few communes in the summer of 1972 to
try and find one to join. The commune in Norfolk was the first one
they stayed at. It was planned that Ernest would work at his job
of lecturing in economics until the Christmas of 1972 before moving
out to live permanently at the commune.

These seven people formed the permanent members of the
commune in the autumn of 1972. The two-and-a-half year's existence
of the commune had seen a fair turnover of members, although none
of the members could hazard any sort of estimation about how many
people had lived there at various times. But, having looked at some
of the paths trodden by those who had come to live at the
commune—how do people come to leave a commune? Where do
they go to? One of the things which the members were agreed upon
was expressed in the following words by Nicholas:

> 'To live here, this has to be your trip. It's not possible to have
> a religious or say, a music trip here. There isn't the peace for
> four hours a day for those who need to practise music. The
> commune itself has to be your main trip.'

Thus, people have generally left to get on with their own thing. Some
have left and have travelled to India, others have left and taken
cottages in the area where they can pursue their interest in music
or whatever. Similarly, a number of couples have left the commune.
As Nicholas described it, 'People who are into each other as couples
tend to want to be together more than they can in the commune.'
One of the members of the commune who had done much of the
electrical work whilst a member, had in fact gone back into a
'straight existence'. He had his hair cut and went back to training
to be an accountant—the members talked of him with great affection
and also some incredulity. They found it difficult to understand
but said they could always justify their existence if they ever
got into trouble with the authorities by claiming to be some sort
of therapeutic community concerned with directing people
who had wandered back on to the 'straight and narrow'—true,
they only had one such 'success' to point to but there might be
more!

Of course not everyone had left the commune completely voluntarily. Not everyone who had sought to become a member had been successful and certain long term visitors had been asked to leave. Who were those who were asked to leave? Well, amongst the limited number who had been asked to leave Dave mentioned the people who were lazy, who didn't know how to work, those who worked for five minutes and then took a tea break. Another time it was someone who worked well but didn't say very much. He irritated certain of the members of the commune just by being himself—he just got on their nerves. Another time some heroin addicts who were very down as they were trying to kick their habit attacked one of the members. They also were asked to leave. People were asked to leave (thrown out) at a meeting of the members at which the individual concerned was present. This process of politely telling someone to move out was not one that was enjoyed by any of the members. Moreover, they worried about selecting members and turning people away. As one of the members put it:

> 'What right have we to turn people away from here when they
> have as much right to the place as we have? We try and
> rationalise it by saying it's not good for the kids to have too
> many people around as the place becomes too crowded for
> them to have space to play in.'

Whilst the members might reject any notion of them having a sovereign right to sole occupation of the property, there was the simple recognition that communes are not for everyone, that some people just cannot get on together and so some selectivity is required in the admission of new permanent members. In the autumn of 1972 there was the feeling that for the first time in the life of the community there was a stable group, they were really together as a group. This had evolved slowly through a process which they described as 'the group selecting itself'. This is simply the process whereby many people who want to become involved in communal living travel round communes looking for a place where they can find the people and the life that suit them. They travel around until they find the place with which they can identify and a group which identifies them as someone who would 'fit in', and so they stay.

Relations with outside

The fact that there are many people wandering around the country-side looking for a place to live, visiting communes and staying for various lengths of time presents many communes with a problem—how to cope with visitors? The commune in Norfolk was made up of a group of individuals who had all travelled along different paths and moved in different circles before coming to the commune. The result was that apart from visitors who came via the addresses supplied by the Commune Movement or who had read of them in *Communes* magazine, they were also visited by people drawn from their different circles of friends. They were also visited by people drawn from the local 'head scene' of Norfolk, such as the four young people who came for an afternoon whilst I was at the commune. They were friends of one of the commune members who had met them at a drug advice centre in the local city. They helped with the garden and with the renovation work during the afternoon and then in the evening sat round the fire with the commune members smoking dope and talking. The commune members themselves saw it as important they were open to visitors such as the people who stayed that afternoon. For them it was a matter of being open to others, so that they could see how the members lived and draw what lessons they could from the experience. It was part of their general attempt to turn others on to alternative ways of living and being. However, visitors did present a problem. There were times when they had to spend so much time relating to the visitors that they didn't have the time or energy to relate to each other, and the group suffered correspondingly. Thus whilst I was there they had a dis-cussion about the coming weekend when they were expecting up to about a dozen people. The question was—should they write and ask these people to postpone their visit or let them come? Nicholas was for putting them off, arguing that it would be a hassle and it would be bad for the kids, they would have no room in which they could play and run about. Jake replied that it would only be a hassle if one thought of it as such. Nicholas argued that it would be alright if visitors busied themselves in the garden and doing jobs outside, but so many visitors just sat around inside the house. The discussion went on for a little while until it was decided that the visitors should come, if only to get it all over with in one hectic weekend rather than postpone it.

Of course the contact that the commune members had with the outside world was not confined to visitors. They were surrounded by their rural neighbours. Relationships with these people appeared to be very good. Early on in the life of the community the local clergyman came round to visit the original members and it seemed that for most of the time that the commune had been in existence at least one of the members had been a regular attender at the local church, either as a member of the congregation or as a member of the church choir. Again, good relations with their neighbours were seen as important as part of their general concern to turn others on. They did not go out to the neighbours and say, 'You should do this and you shouldn't do that,' but at the same time they felt that there was a general awareness amongst their neighbours of what they were trying to do and the life style that they had adopted, although they also felt that many of their neighbours thought that they were mad. However, they drank occasionally at the local pub, some of them went to church regularly, two of their children went to the local village school, they ran a stall at one of the local fêtes, and they helped the local farmer out when he needed extra labour at such times as harvest. The local farmer in turn loaned them his tractor when they needed it, for such things as collecting the off-cuts from the forestry commission which served as fuel for the community during the winter months. This cost them £1 a tractor load. The fact that they had such good relations with their neighbours was at least partly attributable to the fact that the parents of one of the original members lived in the vicinity. Moreover, they formed a useful emergency labour supply for the local farmer whenever he needed them. In addition it has been my experience that many country folk have a certain amount of admiration for anyone, no matter what their appearance, who appears to be making a serious effort to live a life close to the land and in harmony with nature.

Just as the fact that such a 'mob of long-haired weirdoes' had such amicable relations with their neighbours might surprise many, the fact that they also appeared to have good working relationships with the local police surprised me. They spoke in warm terms of their local policeman and claimed that they had suffered virtually no harassment from the various arms of the law. Given the fact that smoking dope was a regular pastime amongst the members of the group I was particularly surprised that they had never been busted.

They had been raided once by the drug squad, but they had been warned by one of the local heads that the police were going round busting everyone, so they had time to get rid of their stuff and race round to one of their neighbours to warn him. Again the situation seemed to be—as in so many areas of Britain—that so long as people are not overtly pushing dope then they are allowed to go on having their quiet smoke without being unduly bothered. It is as if a working relationship is established which is upset only if one of the smokers breaks the rules of the game or else if a representative of the state from outside the area who does not know of, or refuses to play, the accepted game enters the scene. Thus, the four visitors who spent some time at the commune whilst I was there spoke of the threat posed by a new drug squad that had arrived in the local city recently and who were moving round the country lending their dubious services to the local constabularies. The prospect of a drugs raid, however, did not appear to bother the members particularly. As they saw it, first of all it would be very difficult to find any dope on the premises as there were so many places around the property where it could be hidden. Second, if the police did find any dope, who would they charge? No one person owned the house, how could the police decide who to charge with possession? Whilst I was at the commune they told me, as an illustration of their good relations with the local police, of the time they had been driving back to the commune one evening in their van when they were stopped by the police who were carrying out a check-up of vehicles. The police asked where they were from. When told of the village they were heading for, the police interjected, 'Oh, you're from the commune are you?' and they passed on without any further trouble.

Given the fact that the members of the commune do see themselves as part of a general movement for social change it might be expected that they would take an active interest in the events of the world around them. In fact they did not take any of the national newspapers on a regular basis and could not, by any stretch of the imagination, be described as actively seeking to keep abreast of the major news stories of the day. They did not possess a television and the one occasion I heard a member listening to their battered old radio whilst working in the house it was tuned in to pop music on Radio 1. At the same time they kept themselves informed of local events and happenings and had talked amongst themselves about getting involved in local campaigns of one sort or another. However, this was something that needed discussion, as most of them eschewed any commitment to political and social change through means of demonstration and other conventional protest tactics. But as individuals, one or two of them had recently joined forces with others in an attempt to disrupt an otter hunt that had taken place in their neighbourhood. They also talked occasionally of attempting some direct action against the A11 along which traffic roared day and night only 400 yards away from the commune, interrupting the peace and quiet of the countryside. The fanciful aim of such a project, as far as I could gather, was to get the highway moved as it was an irritant to them. At the same time there was the feeling that such a major trunk road symbolised much of the rush, haste, and competitiveness which they had sought to leave behind by moving into the country.

As the commune in Norfolk was associated with the Commune Movement which has as one of its aims the establishment of a federation of communes throughout the world, I was interested to find out what kinds of links, if any, the group had with other communes in the region. They were on friendly terms with a couple of other ventures in the area, but were not involved in any formalised exchange of goods and services or personnel with them—the situation was rather one of occasional visits for a day between the different groups. As for the Commune Movement itself, they felt that the secretaries tended to get involved in their own bureaucratic power struggles, and this disillusioned them. They had been to one of the Commune Movement's 'gatherings' but had returned from this disappointed because they had felt that the 'get-together' had been ruined by a couple of people who insisted on dominating the discussion groups and who didn't even live in a commune themselves. At the same time, the commune had contributed articles to *Communes* magazine which contained practical advice for those who wanted to actually form a commune rather than just talk about it. When it became a matter of someone from the press or from one of the other forms of mass media wanting to do an article or take a film of the group, the members of the commune were reluctant to grant them access. Partly this stemmed from a belief that the richness and variety of life led by the group could not be conveyed in a single article or film. Also, however, their distrust of the media and their motives caused them to turn such people away. It was felt that the glossy magazines and such like only succeeded in turning whatever phenomenon they happened to be covering into yet another commodity to be presented to the consumer market for their consideration—'Here are some funny freaks living in a strange way—everyone look at the funny creatures.' Moreover, some of the members could remember an article on the commune run by one of the local papers which cast a very biased light upon the way of life there—it talked of 'tall, thin, long-haired blond hippies' and of the filth and the squalor of the house. This caused them to be very wary of any members of the press. At the same time they felt that they ought to be open to those who were genuinely interested in their way of life and who they felt would present a fair and appreciative picture of them.

Internal organisation

As one might have expected with a group of people who shared similar ideas, who 'dug living together', and whose expansion of numbers since their beginning had been slow and limited, there was an almost complete absence of any formal, written rules in the commune. In fact when I asked one of the people living there whether they had any rules or not, he thought for a while and then said, 'Well, we did decide a while back that we were spending too much money on dope and so we decided not to buy any more for a time, but we've bought some since then for Sid's birthday.' This was the nearest he could come to providing me with an example of a rule at the commune. True, there were scribbled notices in the kitchen telling you in which coloured buckets to put the various types of waste that were left after the meal—clean greens in the blue bucket for the goat, silver paper in another bucket and so on. There was also a little note telling the reader how to clean and treat the wooden bowls out of which the meals were generally eaten. Other than these guidelines for action there were no formalised, written-down rules of any sort. This is not to say that there were no conventional ways of doing things within the commune—rather there were no agreed-upon and written-down or openly articulated sets of instructions and guidelines or injunctions which existed to direct the individual's activities and the relationships within the community. In this sense the commune was completely open. It had not always been so. There used to be a rule that anyone who wanted to smoke, straight cigarettes or dope, had to stand in the large fireplace so that the smoke went up the chimney. This rule was set by a couple who suffered with asthma and who claimed that the smoke upset them. Those days passed when the couple left the commune. By late 1972 there was not even the minimal kind of formal organisation that one would expect such as a roster for the cooking of meals, washing up, etc.

How did everyday chores get done then? How did they manage to get a meal cooked twice a day? The simple answer is that such things did get done by whoever decided to do them. Whilst such a practice meant that meal times varied a great deal, it did ensure that the members were not ruled and constrained by some structure which was originally intended to facilitate an orderly arrangement of life. They were not governed by some impersonal creation of their own, their sense of freedom was maintained even at the cost of the occasional rumbling stomach. Usually it happened that someone who had not made the meal for a while would decide to do it, although naturally enough this task tended to fall upon certain members with more frequency than it did upon others. However, one day during my stay at the commune nobody had made a move to start preparing the evening meal by seven o'clock. People were feeling rather tired and hungry. The person who had made the meal the evening before asked out loud, 'Who's going to get tea ready?' Dave said that he didn't want to do it because he had been baking all day and was feeling tired. Time passed and there was occasional discussion on this theme of who was to get tea ready. Eventually, as two of the men had left to visit the pub at the end of the lane, Dave and Sid ended up making the meal. As for such chores as cleaning the house, when I first arrived at the commune I was surprised to find the interior of the house so clean and tidy. It was explained to me that the father of one of the members was spending the night with them, and while the rest of the commune had taken the children to the local city for the afternoon the remaining members had taken the opportunity of giving the place a good clean out. On another occasion a member might decide that the place was looking particularly untidy and dirty and just set about cleaning up himself. Certainly, the commune would never win a competition for cleanliness and tidiness, but then none of the members would ever think of entering such a competition.

To say that there were no formalised rules in the commune does not mean to say that group decisions were not made. I was surprised how many areas of life appeared to call for a group decision.

For instance, whilst I was there one of the members had a bath. Afterwards, in the communal living area whilst he was trying to brush his long hair, he suggested that the commune ought to buy a new hair brush. There were about four members present and they each voiced their opinion on this matter. The general consensus that emerged was that the commune should not buy a new hair brush, although if someone wanted to steal one that was a different matter. The one with the wet straggly hair bowed out gracefully. Another incident illustrated the manner in which decisions were made in the community. The commune had just taxed their van which was provided for them by Ernest who would join the community as a permanent member after he finished his job at Christmas as an economics lecturer. He naturally had taken a special interest in the financial arrangements of the commune, and he and David, who was learning the basic book-keeping skills with him, were discussing the question of vehicle insurance. They realised that Nicholas was not covered by their insurance policy as he had not passed his driving test. During the course of the meal David announced, 'Have you heard our decision—Nicholas is not to drive the van until he gets a licence.' At this Nicholas's 'wife' demanded to know what right David had to make a decision like that. Who had been consulted? Had a commune meeting been called? No meeting had been called. Her response was, 'Shall we have a meeting about it now—O.K.?' They set to over the meal table discussing the question of whether Nicholas should drive the van or not. Eventually it was decided that he should not drive the van until he had passed his driving test. The crucial argument that determined this decision was the prospect of the disastrous consequences for the commune if he should be involved in an accident whilst not covered by insurance and the commune as a whole was sued for damages. The question of whether it was legal or illegal for Nicholas to drive whilst formally unqualified did not arise at all.

Just as Ernest with his experience of economics and accounting had taken a special interest in the financial arrangements of the commune, so other members tended to take a special interest in certain areas of communal life. What this meant was that although the members did not recognise any formal division of labour within the group, and in fact consciously tried to avoid any such specialisation of function developing, at the same time certain members tended to have areas of expertise. Thus, Dave was the member who knew most about building and construction work. Sid was the one who knew most about gardening. However, he had got fed up with gardening and just prior to my visit had stopped working in the garden, with the result that the weeds had taken hold by the time the other members got around to noticing and trying to rescue the remainder of their plot and prepare it for the next year's vegetable crop. Apart from such 'specialisms', one of the women was beginning to take a special responsibility for the hens, whilst it appeared to me that Jake took a particular interest in feeding and milking their British Alpine goat. Having gathered from crofter neighbours that cows and goats like to be milked at regular times by the same person I asked Jake about whether the milking was in fact his special area of expertise. Evidently this particular issue was a point of disagreement at that time within the commune—Jake and Dave felt that one person should look after the goat, whilst Nicholas and others felt that everyone should play their part in caring for it, arguing that if any of the members did not involve themselves with each aspect of the communal activities including milking the goat, then they would forget about that side of the communal life. They would not be involving themselves as fully as possible in the commune's life. The big thing was the group, the commune, and any specialisation of tasks and division of labour on a permanent basis would be against this. I agreed with Jake that whilst this attitude was all well and good for many things, it represented a lack of concern for the feelings of the poor goat which would inevitably be milked at different times and in different ways by different people on different days—a goat needs a secure cosmos if it is to produce milk.

The major source of income of the commune was derived from the sale of their home-baked fruit loaves. About 90 of these unleavened loaves were baked each week for delivery to London. In the earlier days of the community everyone had joined in making them at the same time. The result was that everyone got in each other's way, and the quality of the fruit loaves suffered. As a consequence they developed a kind of division of labour over time. That is, they took weekly turns at making the fruit loaves. With a limited number of members, the organisation of this task was merely a question of deciding early on each week whose turn it was to make the fruit-breads that week, and then leaving that person to get on with it as and when he or she felt like it.

Just as within a commune of only eight members there is little need for any formalised system of rule-making or any impersonal means of communication between the members, the members of the commune in Norfolk did not have any special group method of dealing with the tensions and inter-personal problems that inevitably accompany any venture into communal living. They did not have anything which they would compare to a group 'encounter session', but there was the feeling that any member of the group who was feeling low for some reason knew that he had people surrounding him with whom he could talk and share his concerns. At the same time, one got the feeling that one or two members would prefer to see attempts established to create something along the lines of regular encounter sessions when the members could open out to each other and confront each other in direct and unmediated fashion.

Apart from the adult members of the commune, there were four children living there, two of whom went to the local village school. To an extent each member of the community took some part in caring for the kids and playing with them. But in practice the two mothers who lived in the community played the greatest role in caring for their kids, preparing them for bed, cleaning them up and so on. This was something that the other members were aware of, however, and about which the male members felt rather guilty. What this meant was that although the commune members did not recognise any sexual division in tasks and duties, in practice the women spent a disproportionate amount of their time compared with the other, male, members caring for their respective children. This was so even though the group as a whole tended to think of itself as a group rather than as separate individuals and couples. Thus, although the two women members of the commune were 'married' to two of the male members, in the case of one of the couples they were definitely not 'together' as a couple, and the woman slept with other commune members. The other couple, Nicholas and Chris, were together as a couple although they also slept with other people. The biological fathers of the children, like their mothers, spent more time with the children than did other members.

Finance

As was remarked above, the property was originally bought by one of the founder members with money he inherited. One of the major problems that faces any communal group that has been in existence for any length of time concerns the question of what happens to the property when those who originally acquired it decide to leave the group. When I first visited the commune in Norfolk the founder member who had bought the property expressed his desire that when the time came for him to move on to do other things, the property itself should be passed on to others who were involved in communal living. At that time he had only the vaguest of ideas how this could be achieved in practice. After two years at the commune, this person left to live with his girlfriend and their child in a neighbouring village and so the problem of property ownership had to be faced. The solution that emerged had been the formation of a non-trading, non-profit making limited company, called under the Companies Acts a 'Company Limited by Guarantee and not having a Share Capital'. The commune members wrote an article for *Communes* outlining their solution to this ownership problem in the hope that their experiences might help others living in communal situations. This is what they wrote:[3]

Shrubb Family found itself in the position where their owner wanted to leave the commune and to sell the house concerned to the commune. He also wanted to ensure that the commune would remain in existence. . . . The commune was basically opposed to involving itself in a great deal of meaningless documentation and the simplest procedure was sought. It did not want the existing communal structure to be imposed upon but rather for it to be reflected in the constitution of the proposed body.

People would be free to come and go; the operation of the commune would not be defined procedurally but would be evolved gradually and be based on tradition; the property would be bought out of the collective income rather than with members' accumulated capital. No fixed formula would be used to decide the amount of money to be given to members leaving, each case being considered separately. . . .

It was decided to form a non-trading, non-profit making limited company for the following reasons:
(a) No matter how many trustees there are of a trust only the first four have legal recognition in the case of property ownership. A private limited company may have between two and fifty members.

E

(*b*) The setting up and operation of a limited company are
simplified matters and can be accomplished without professional
assistance. . . .

(*c*) The members of the commune would be the members of
the company and they would be protected in the event of the
company being wound up by having limited liability . . . the
limit of each member's liability . . . in the case of a company
limited by guarantee . . . is the amount each member
guarantees to pay in the event of the company being wound
up. . . .

It was decided to form a 'company limited by guarantee' . . .
merely to own the property and run the commune. The
company would have a nominal director and secretary and the
amount of each member's guarantee would be five new pence.

If any businesses are developed by the commune these will
be separate from the company and will be the legal responsibility
of individual members. When it becomes necessary to combine
and incorporate them a second limited company will be
formed . . . a wholly owned subsidiary of the original (holding)
company. Each business will have its own department. . . .

With Shrubb Family the total income is pooled and the
house will be paid for as a normal expense out of this fund. In
a few years' time the commune will own the house and
succeeding members will be able to come and go without any
need for new members to bring large sums of money with them.

Many communes of the past used to have rules about potential
members contributing all their wordly wealth into the communal
pool. This was something which in practice seemed to happen at the
Norfolk commune but which was not formally required of new
members. Thus, when Val and Ernest joined the group they put all
their savings and the money they received from the sale of their
home in London into the commune. This sum amounted to somewhere in the region of £4,000. Nicholas and Chris, on the other hand,
had no money to contribute into the common pool when they joined.
David had no money when he originally joined but during his stay
he received a small inheritance which he used to return to Australia.
On his return to the commune he put the remainder of his
inheritance, about £400, into the common pool. The commune,
however, did have a rule concerning money which a person might

have as savings and capital which he or she did not contribute into
the common pool. This was simply that if a person possessed private
capital then they must not draw upon it for their personal use. This
was a safeguard against the problems and tensions that would arise
if the commune members as individuals possessed different levels of
income, some having ready money to spend on various things and
others having little or nothing.

The total income of the commune was pooled. During the autumn
of 1972 this money was derived from two major sources. From the
sale of their fruit-breads they obtained about £16 a week profit
after they had paid for the ingredients. In addition Ernest
contributed his income that he obtained from lecturing. This latter
source of finance would dry up when Ernest became a full-time
member in 1973. They estimated roughly that they spent about
£25 a week on running expenses such as food, fuel, tobacco and so
on. The previous winter a number of them had worked outside the
commune peeling onions at a local factory. None of them enjoyed
this work but they anticipated that in the future they might have to
resort to outside work of this sort when they no longer received the
monthly salary from Ernest. During my stay at the commune they
were in the process of trying to estimate with some degree of
accuracy how much money they spent each week on what kinds of
items. They had started keeping detailed accounts of their income
and expenditure. The commune had a cheque book which could be
used by all the members. As much of their food-stuff as possible was
bought in bulk as well as the ingredients used for making the fruit-
breads. The fruit-breads were sold in London to a whole-food
restaurant and to the public through a shop known as Community
Services. This shop operated as a sales outlet for the produce of
communes and groups around the country, the owner merely adding
around 10 per cent to the retail price to cover his expenses. Since the
commune was trying to be self-sufficient, trying to live outside the
capitalist system as much as possible, they tried to sell as much of
their produce as possible through Community Services rather than
to the whole-food restaurant which was run on a conventional
money-making basis. Although they allowed for a profit in the price
that they charged for their fruit-breads, one of the members estimated that if one worked out the hours spent on making them (they
were baked in batches of about nine) it worked out at a 'wage rate'
of only ten pence an hour. In fact they charged the restaurant more

for the fruit-breads than they charged the 'head shop'. Basically they did not like selling their produce to 'money-makers'. As they were in a fairly comfortable economic position whilst they received Ernest's monthly contribution, in so far as they had money in the 'kitty', the question was raised by one of the members during my stay that they should give away that week's batch of fruit-breads rather than sell them. By giving their produce away they would, in some small measure, be subverting the existing exchange relationships between producer and consumer. Nevertheless I felt obliged to ask them why they should want to do such a thing. The answer was simple and straightforward: ' 'Cos it's a nice thing to do, that's why.'

The commune had a kind of petty cash box which the members drew from when they went shopping and so on. If any visitor insisted upon making a financial contribution to the commune, a contribution which would not be asked for, then it was to this petty cash box that they would be directed to leave whatever they felt they wanted to donate.

Daily routine

As one would expect from a group of people who were consciously seeking to live a way of life completely different from that led by the majority of folk in society, a life which many had chosen as a consequence of their experiences of the boring routine of nine till five work, there were no set rules of the commune about what time one should start work, at what time one should have a tea break, etc. As with so many things, the hours a person spent working or sleeping or whatever was an individual thing. One member, for instance, got up at six o'clock in the morning when it was his week for making the fruit-breads. Others stayed in bed much later, getting up when the spirit moved them. This could be well on into the morning. Each member had his own room, although those who were together as couples naturally tended to sleep together. They also naturally seemed to be the people who stayed in bed longer in a morning. Breakfast was an individual affair. Whoever got up first might make a pan of porridge for whoever might like some. Otherwise people just helped themselves as and when they got up to a breakfast which might include coffee, home-made muesli, home-made unleavened bread and honey, or the ever-present fruit-bread. The morning itself might be spent on any of the jobs that occupy the time of any rural communal group, working in the garden, working on the renovation and conversion of the house, cleaning the house, making the fruit-breads, preparing the mid-day meal, going shopping or just sitting around talking and smoking. The mid-day meal was taken together and like the evening meal was often preceded by a period of silence when the people around the table all held hands and meditated silently for a short while. The meals themselves were vegetarian, and most of the members ate with chopsticks out of wooden bowls. The food itself obviously varied with the season and what the garden and the shops could provide. Jerusalem artichokes seemed to form a staple part of the diet during my stay. The afternoons were typically spent in a similar manner to the mornings, people working or else sitting around talking, listening to records, having a smoke, or whatever. Following the evening meal during the winter months people sat around the large wood fire, one of them might play the piano whilst the others sang along or got on with reading, sewing, or doing whatever they had to do. One thing that surprised me, however, was that when the members retired to bed they kissed each other on the lips as they wished each other good night. For one brought up in the conventional English household where physical touch between people, particularly oral contact, is kept to a minimum, this came as something of a surprise. However, one noticeable thing about life at the commune was the degree of physical touch and contact that went on between the members. The people there were regularly throwing their arms round each other, hugging and embracing each other, kissing each other, sitting on each other's laps and so on. Whilst outside a commune one would find such behaviour strange and 'queer', within the commune it all seemed perfectly natural, and to me at least it symbolised the closeness that existed between the members of the group, the feeling of warmth that each had for one another—a large but close-knit family.

Problems and future prospects

Just as with any family, however, life in a commune has its problems and its hang-ups. One problem faced by the group in Norfolk was the imbalance of the ratio of women to men. There were two women and six men. They would have liked more women to join them in their life. This would be a big step for any woman to make on her own however, and they had been unsuccessful in their search.

Nicholas and Chris, prior to joining the commune, had lived together as a couple and had a small child. During the course of my stay Nicholas described their relationship in terms which seemed to imply that although they still thought of themselves as a couple, they did sleep with other people. Enquiring of another member as to whether sexual jealousy cropped up as a problem within the commune, he replied, 'Sure, Nicholas and Christine are discovering that now.'

In fact, a commune such as this does not seem to be the place where two people who are very close to each other as a monogamous couple will find what they are searching for. Couples present communes such as Norfolk with real problems. As one of the members expressed it:

> 'The commune has not changed in its direction over time, but it has become better. The people here now are very much into living with each other. Those into other things, like monogamous couples, have left. One of the problems of couples is that they tend to lean on each other. If there is any disagreement amongst the commune members over something, then inevitably the couple cling together and form a bloc.'

This was something I noticed when it was suggested that Nicholas should no longer drive the commune's van. Immediately it was Christine who jumped to his defence, wanting to know why this should be so. Didn't they realise how much they had depended on Nicholas driving the van in the past? Who else would be willing to do the weekly 'bread run' down to London if Nicholas could not do it? Moreover, to the extent that a couple are very close and want time to themselves to do things together, then communes, such as at Norfolk, where things were done on an individual or group basis and where everyone was living together in such a close and intense fashion are not the place for them.

This problem of being alone, of finding the time and the space within a commune to be quiet and enjoy a bit of privacy, was not one that particularly bothered the members of the Norfolk commune. For individuals who wished to be alone, they could retire to their room or they could go off on their own for a walk in the country. Other members adopted different strategies. Thus, one of the members used to get up early in the morning before anyone else had stirred in order to enjoy a few hours of peace and quiet before the house filled up with people, noise and activity.

Of course, not everybody can live a life led in close proximity with others. Even within the small, 'self-selected' group at the commune in Norfolk there were times when individual members would get on the nerves of other members. There were times when a person would feel low and 'edgy', when he didn't feel like being friendly and relating to the others. The answer that the members had to the problem was the same solution that most married couples have to develop—'you have to learn tolerance.' Particularly, you have to learn tolerance and everyday wisdom to see you through the early hours of the day. It is at this time that people, even people in communes, are at their touchiest. Thus, one of the petty problems at the commune in Norfolk was that by the time most of the people were getting up, the early riser had been up and about for a few hours, was full of life and full of conversation. This could be irritating for those who were desperately trying to throw off the effects of the night before and the hours of sleep. 'You have to learn tolerance.'

In a commune such as in Norfolk where there was a genuine feeling of warmth, love and concern felt by the members for each other, when one of the members was feeling low and down for some reason then the others would spend a lot of their energy trying to get the individual high again. This meant that their energy was going into this rather than into work on the garden or on the building, and consequently the work didn't get done. One of the problems faced by the commune was this very thing that sometimes as a group they didn't seem to have any energy to do things. They just sat around all day without being able to get themselves sufficiently together to get out and work. This problem was related to another one. Just as in a marriage it can be very difficult for one partner to remain buoyant and happy when the other partner is feeling miserable and low, so in the commune they had found that if one of their number was feeling down and negative, then this soon spread to the other members of the group and before long everyone was feeling depressed.

Whilst the rewards for those who live in the commune were seen in terms of living a richer life in terms of self-development than would otherwise be possible, there are obvious constraints upon the individual entailed in living communally. As has been remarked, there was the feeling that to live at the commune the commune itself has to be your 'thing'. As one member said:

> 'If you live here all your energy is spent on the group—there is no room for individual trips. You are making fruit-loaves, cooking, repairing the house and so on. Everything you do is for the group.'

So, as has been remarked, many of the people who left had done so in order to get on with their own individual trip, whether this was music, painting, religion or whatever. However, there were other kinds of constraints. You are constrained about the money you spend, because all the time you have to think of all the other members. This was felt particularly strongly by the two older members who had held steady, well-paid jobs for some years prior to joining the commune. As Sid remarked:

> 'I find it difficult to get out of this habit of spending money. For twelve years I always had money to spend—mainly on rubbish. Ernest finds the same problem as well—he's always had money to buy things when he wanted them. It's easier for the others who have never had money to spend.'

In fact, because the members of the commune were receiving a monthly salary from Ernest, shortage of finance was not a major problem for them at that time during my stay. They felt that in the future, when Ernest had finished working, they would experience financial depressions. But they did not worry about this. Like the people at Findhorn[4] they felt that if you had faith, then things would work out right. They quoted the example of the founder member of the commune going on holiday to Austria at a time when they were looking for an architect to design their conversion of the building. Whilst on holiday he met an architect who offered his services—they had the architect they needed. If things did get financially tight, then they felt that some of them could go out to work outside the community, but this would be a last resort. Most of their future plans, when they thought about them—and in fact they did not think about the future much but tried to live in the present—centred upon developments in terms of the garden and the conversion of the building. They hoped to build a quiet meditation room for the commune. They also looked forward to getting an extra communal living room ready which could perhaps be set aside for the children. They also hoped to reduce their reliance upon the 'system' by increasing their self-sufficiency. Thus, they were considering the possibility of creating their own methane fuel from compost and waste. In terms of future projections about the numbers living there, they felt that the size of the building and the garden would not allow them to expand their numbers greatly. However, some of them felt that it would be good to move to a larger place eventually. The problem was that to buy a larger place they would need the money obtained from the sale of their existing property, but as they would not want to sell their property on the open market but would want to pass it on to another communal group, this would deny them the opportunity of raising the necessary funds to buy the new property. This conflict between their desire to aid other groups and their concern for their own well-being is one that they will have to resolve in the future. In the meantime their problems are of a somewhat more mundane character, as the poem written by one of the members indicates:

> Greetings to all you commune freaks outside
> This is an Easter message from the wide
> And open spaces north of Cambridge where
> No motorways pollute the rural air—
> Merely a friendly lane (the A.11)
> Winds comfortably close to Shrubb Farm Heaven.

> Our goats are milkless but we get of late
> An extra pint of cow's milk from the State,
> Our eggless free range hens have gone, and yet
> Ten thousand hens lay on across the Thet,
> Our fruitcakes net us £20 or more;
> Yet car, cakes and accounting keep us poor.
> Our unsprayed plot might give us all we need
> In herb and pulse and root and leaf and seed;
> But bindweed sprouts, and, lodgers love to sleep
> And labour's loath, and poisoned veg are cheap.

> No paradox or irony implied—
> Merely that Mother Nature loves to chide
> Her guileless lovers. Milk and eggs and pence
> And veg will come with love's experience.

Chapter 4

Kingsway Community

A Christian therapeutic commune; an extended family

Origins and beliefs

The natural ability of man to live through co-operation with others has, in each one of us, become injured and become invalid, and this because of a condition of fear in a society run on a 'competitive' basis as our society is.

We do not wish to adapt to this society, to accept that condition.

Rather, we intend to create a society, moved and sustained by the example of Christ, in which we deal with each other as brothers and sisters. We do not want our actions to be variations in a manner of bargaining; we will give attention to others not because it is to our personal advantage, not because we will get something out of it, but simply as we have life in us.

As brothers and sisters we recognise that it is our Father's will— it is in the nature of earth—for all our needs to be covered. Therefore, we repudiate the mere financial structure of society, and we work to give food and shelter and fellowship, as rights, to our neighbours in need. And working together in the service of Christ we are serviceable one to another, and bold to heal and recreate society.

This was the guiding belief and outlook which led David Horn to found the Kingsway Community in West London some years ago. He had come up from North Devon to study at the Royal College of Art in London. In many ways it was London itself that set David along the path towards community. As he expressed it to me, before coming up to London he had read Aldous Huxley's *Brave*

New World and thought that things might well appear to be moving in such a direction, but when he arrived in London he found that this anti-utopia was already a reality there. A Christian, who believed that it was not enough to be a 'Christian for five minutes a day', but that one must live one's whole life according to Christian precepts, he saw how pointless and ineffective it was being the 'Good Samaritan' and giving the beggar the shilling he asked for, and then walking off leaving him in exactly the same situation, except that he now had a shilling in his pocket. The Christian must open his door to his neighbour, he must consider others' needs as his own, see that the welfare of his neighbour is his own welfare. So he opened his door to the 'social inadequates', the dossers, and the lonely. He and his wife obtained two adjacent flats in west London in which they were joined by up to about half a dozen others. Numbers grew so that in 1969 they took over the lease of a large house with a garden in west London.

The basic idea behind the community was to create a Christian community, an extended family, to care for those in need, the oppressed and the sick. Technically, it was hoped that this would be achieved through the establishment of a nucleus of about seven Christians, committed to the ideal of a Christian community, who would then be able to form the 'hard core' of the extended family. David Horn has expressed it as follows:[1]

It is achieved [the community], technically, by establishing an extended family. At least two couples and several friends take up the rooms suitable to their separate needs in a house: then there are at least three women to share the workaday life, and there is sufficient income. Everyone puts into the kitty such money as he can. Any money surplus to the week's spending is given to the Church; the Church owns the house, and administers money wherever it is called for, and connects ailing households with the strong. This group of people living together, having security only in fellowship, are sufficiently resourceful as to provide for their neighbours—whoever is in need. Some who are homeless will complete the family group, which will keep an open door, a common table, and a dormitory, so that others may have their basic needs supplied until the next community house is opened. Every community will differ according to its members and its locality but together they will be a recreated society.

Recruitment and members

When I first visited the house in the summer of 1970 it held about thirty-six people of whom about seven considered themselves to be Christians. The house held up to fifty people on some occasions, the number of temporary visitors depending to some extent on the weather conditions and whether it was warm enough to sleep outside or not. Apart from David, his wife and two young children, and a number of others who could be said to form the stable core of the house, the other members were made up of drug addicts, alcoholics, people just out of prison with no place to go and people who had just been led there because they had no roof over their heads and no friends to lean on. From talking to people at the community one could construct a typical story of how people came to start living at the house. Arriving in London from Ireland or the provinces, either a drug addict, in trouble with the police, just out of prison, or some other form of 'social misfit', without money or food, and homeless, eventually hearing about the existence of the house and the possibility of getting a roof over one's head there and also something to eat—so they arrived and many of them stayed. When I visited the community in 1970 one of the members estimated that there were probably six to eight drug addicts in the house, a couple of alcoholics, and the bulk of the others were people who had come to the house having left home and arrived in London with no money, food or job, and been directed there by knowledgeable members of the less fashionable 'underground' of the London scene, or by a social worker or priest.

After my first visit I kept in touch with David and I returned to the community in October 1972. My first impressions on arrival were that the house itself seemed much cleaner and better equipped than on my first visit. A stroll round the garden revealed other changes. An attempt was being made to develop a small vegetable garden and in the corner of the back garden there was a small hen coop with three brown hens scratching around. I discovered that these provided the community with about a dozen eggs a week. Changes had also taken place in the numbers and composition of the commune membership. David was still there and had not changed much, but his wife had left the community. She had suffered a breakdown in her health and had gone to live with her mother in Oxfordshire where David visited her whenever he could afford the time. However, David had been joined by Brian who had come to the community as a house worker and was helping to take some of the responsibility and burden of running the house off David's shoulders. Brian had come to London from Ireland to complete his training as a surveyor. He had learnt of the community from his brother, a parish priest in Ireland. He visited and decided that this was the life he was looking for as an alternative to the pursuance of his professional career. He packed in his studies and came to the community. Apart from this addition, the number of members had declined significantly from when I had made my initial visit. From the time when the house had up to fifty people sleeping there, the number in residence on my second visit had declined to around twenty or so. The fact that the house seemed much cleaner and tidier reflected this decline in numbers and the fact that the community now had a fairly stable group membership. The decline in numbers reflected a compromise that the members of the community had reluctantly arrived at between their desire to have an open door for all those who were in need and the realisation that everyone living in the community needed help and assistance of some form or another. When numbers got around the mid-forties the place became so crowded and congested that people had no time or energy to care for each other, with the result that the open-door policy meant that no-one was getting any help at all.

In 1970 it had seemed that anyone without a roof over their head could turn to the Kingsway Community for a place to stay until they managed to find a place of their own. By 1972 this policy had been tightened up in the light of the considerations just referred to. A rule had emerged at one of the house meetings that people could only stay for one night, after which they must make some financial contribution towards the house and it would be left up to the residents to decide as to how long they could stay. I saw this rule at work during my stay. Pat, an Irishman, who seemed to be in his early 60s, but who could have been younger, had spent one night at the community. He was working in the neighbourhood but had been unable to find anywhere to stay. The previous week he had spent two nights sleeping out in freezing weather in a local park. He was a really nice, quiet, friendly man who appeared to be on friendly terms with the other members whom he knew from when he had stayed at the community on odd occasions before. During the evening meal David raised the issue of Pat. He had stayed one night and the house rule was that people could only crash for one night. What was to be the house decision? Pat was sitting in the room at the time and no-one said anything. Eventually one of the long-term members, a young mother, said in a soft voice that he should be allowed to stay that night, his second, but that was all. David repeated this aloud to the others present at the table asking for comments on this proposal. All he got in reply were murmurs. He took the lack of response as assent and announced it as the house decision. Sitting next to Pat I asked him where he would stay the next night. He did not know but supposed it would be the park again. We were sitting on a couch and on his knee he was bouncing the baby of one of the couples in the community. He turned to me and said, 'One thing about kids, they don't care who you are. The only problem is that they have to grow up.' He didn't appear bitter about the decision. Just sad and resigned. 'It's a shitty world when this sort of thing can happen to a nice old man', I thought—here he was sitting quietly playing with a laughing baby on his knee in a warm room and tomorrow he would be sleeping on some park bench on his own somewhere.

This is the problem with communes when they make rules. There is always a marginal case that is crying out and demanding to be made the exception, and this is why David had received no reply to his request for opinions about Pat—people knew the house decision about overnight stays, but who would be the one to speak out publicly and so have on his conscience that it was he who could be deemed responsible for the plight of one of his fellow men? After about five minutes one of the commune members, Blue, from Birmingham who had come to the community from a mental hospital, and who did not speak or communicate with people much, blurted out, 'Why shouldn't Pat stay—I've got nothing against him?' All that David could reply to this was to point out that they had the house rule and the house had just come to its decision. No one else was prepared to speak out and the decision stood. I was left thinking what right have I to criticise when I spend my time living with my wife, two dogs and cats in a three-bedroomed house surrounded by the beautiful scenery of Garioch in Aberdeenshire? What right have I to criticise those who are seeking to maintain a 'homely' atmosphere which, for many, must be their first experience of a genuine family relationship with others?

It could not be said that Pat had been thrown out of the community, as he knew the rules before he came. Others had been thrown out, however. Generally the people who had been 'evicted' had been those who were either too disruptive and aggressive, who upset all the other members of the house so that they were denied any personal benefit to their health or stability by that person's presence in the house, or else those who continually flouted the 'agreement' which the house had decided new members should agree to abide by when they entered the community. This agreement, formalised on 20 September 1972 read as follows:

At a meeting between the Hackney and Chiswick full-time workers the agreement made by the members of the Chiswick household was examined and adopted in the form set down below. THE DEMANDS the members of the Kingsway Community make on each other become greater, more exacting, as we repudiate the forces which promote our self-interest or that divide in order to control us, as we build a society founded upon co-operation and a common welfare. These notes indicate the necessary commitment of each member.

THE FIRST PRINCIPLE is that food is common; the main daily meal is the central act of sharing, and to partake is the unfailing requirement made of everyone who would belong to an extended family in the Community.

IT FOLLOWS THAT everyone is required to take their part in preparing the meals, in clearing and cleaning and maintaining their house, personal and common areas alike.

The week's routine includes a house-meeting—to attend, and to abide by decisions reached in debate during that meeting, is required of everyone; and an outing.

Events organised in the common-room have priority over the television even in houses where there is a room set apart for television. There is to be no more than one television, owned by the household.

Each household forms an agreement as to the minimal financial contribution everyone is to make to the household purse, while remembering that a full commitment will enable one to pool all income and to take out what one needs.

While it is necessary for some members to be in employment they would not enter for its own sake, it is a vital corollary to the establishment of an extended family that it should provide meaningful work itself. (An industry is gradually being built up from the workshop in Chiswick.)

Anyone registered as a drug-addict consents, as a member of the household, to a house-worker taking full reponsibility for the drugs, collecting and administering them as prescribed by the clinic. For this purpose a safe is to be used by the house-workers. Illegal drug abuse is a matter for internicine concern: the smoking of hashish cannot take place in our households if only because of the dynamics of such groups; more personal and obsessive drug-abuse needs as much control as the group can exert.

As the life and the development of the Community depends on the recognition of our neighbour's right to food, shelter and fellowship, each household is bound to be hospitable.

Thus, people who made no attempt to display any commitment to the community, who never attended the evening meal, who were rarely to be seen around the place, who paid no financial contribution into the house funds and treated the community merely as somewhere to stay on odd occasions—these constituted one group of people who were asked to leave the community to make way for others. As far as I could gather this was only a rare occurrence, people were warned of the feeling of the house, usually by David, and given every opportunity to display a minimal commitment to the 'agreement'.

The other types of person who had been asked to leave in the past were the extremely violent and aggressive members who had managed repeatedly to disrupt the life of the community. One such person was the husband of one of the members and the father of her child. He was repeatedly causing fights and dominated his wife to the extent that she was not deriving any benefit from her membership of the community.

Another change in the recruitment and membership policy of the community reflected the problems that had accrued to the group as a result of providing a home for up to about half a dozen drug addicts at any one time. The practice in the autumn of 1972 was that the community only housed one or two addicts at one time. Only a few minutes after my arrival at the community for the second time a conversation I was involved in with Brian was interrupted by David who informed him that one of the two addicts that had been living in the house had just been discovered dead in his bed. This person had been abusing his body for years with barbiturates and David informed me that it was a miracle that he had lived as long as he had done. He was in his early twenties—he had died of an 'exhausted body and an exhausted mind'.[2] It had been found that when the community had any significant number of addicts living there they tended to form their own closed sub-group within the community, centred round their drug deals and use, to which entry was denied to anyone else. As such they only served to reinforce each other's habit and although when one of them fell out with the rest of the group the other members of the community felt that they could make contact and relate with him, this contact was severed once he had re-established his relationships with the other addicts again. Thus it was felt that it would be better for the community and better for the individual addicts if their numbers were reduced to just one or two.

Relations with outside

Although the numbers who were members of the Kingsway Community had declined with the passage of time as part of a conscious policy, the community itself had developed a number of other 'arms'.

The community had its origins with the personal commitment of David and his wife. They had received very little assistance from any other charities or the churches, although the community had a tenuous link with the Methodist church and promises of help and assistance had come from these quarters, particularly from the West London Mission with which Lord Soper is associated. Indeed the community had been promised the finance necessary to purchase additional property by Lord Soper and the West London Mission if David could gather around him a Christian hardcore that would act as a nucleus and ensure that the community was run according to Christian principles. However, by late 1972 the only practical assistance that had been provided from these sources had largely been confined to putting in a good word for the community in the right ear when the need arose. However, a group called 'Friends of Kingsway Community' had formed itself. Its members were drawn from the Chiswick area of London and were described by David as 'radicals who have marched for peace in their time but are now feeling slack and want to do something'. This group, amongst whose

F

members was to be found a local JP, had proved of great assistance
to the community as a support group who took a great deal of the
administrative burden off David's shoulders. This group had prepared the way for the community to achieve the legal status of a
housing association. This support group, then, was one arm of the
community.

Another was the Hackney house referred to in the agreement.
This house had its immediate origins with a group of people who had
worked with the Cyrenians and who contacted David with a view
to developing a residential home for drug addicts. David was in a
position to help them as, in his own words, he had 'been softening
the Greater London Council up for some time about the possibility
of getting another house'. They managed to obtain a house in
Hackney with the specific purpose of housing addicts. However,
David himself was rather critical of this additional arm of the
Kingsway Community. He felt that it had too small and narrow a
membership base, confined as it was to addicts. Also, he was particularly upset by the distinction that had developed there between
the two groups of members—the people living there had started
distinguishing between the 'house workers' and the 'residents'.
This categorising of people was 'invidious', he felt, merely serving
to create the kinds of barriers between people that inevitably accompanied any attempt to care for others that took place within the
confines of the 'social worker' and his or her 'client'.

Another arm of the community which had appeared since 1970
was the house that they had in Devon at Bridford. This cottage had
been provided by someone involved with the church who had heard
of the community and offered them the property on permanent
loan. It housed half a dozen people, some of whom had gone there
from the community in London. There was some talk about the
house at Bridford, at the London community during my stay. The
members there had all become involved in the Divine Light Mission
and wanted to turn the community into an *ashram*. David himself
did not mind if they did turn it into an *ashram*, as he felt that there
was room for specifically religious communities, so long as membership was not made exclusive to members of the Divine Light Mission.

Apart from these developments, the community at Kingsway was
still waiting for what was felt to be its most significant project to get
under way. Back in 1970 members of the community had been
anticipating a move to a farm on Exmoor, but by January 1971 they

had missed their chance due to their failure to raise the necessary capital in time. For a long time there had been the desire on the part of David and other members to 'get back to nature' and to develop a self-sufficient rural commune in which everyone would contribute through work and income and where addicts and people like them who were trying to break with their habits and their urban haunts could start to get themselves together. David had written some years before: 'For those who would serve Him the community farm will be a seminary. For those who are destroying themselves in the city it will offer life renewed.' The disappointment experienced when they failed to get the farm on Exmoor was only the first set-back of many in their search for suitable rural property. By late 1972 there was a certain element of desperation felt by those looking forward to the move to the country—there was the feeling of 'How long can we hold out in the city before we manage to get out into the country?'

Fortunately for the community, they had attracted the support and sympathy of a London businessman with a special interest in drug addiction. He had literally picked up an addict in Soho one day and someone had told him to take the addict, who was in poor shape, to the Kingsway community. Met by David they got into conversation and David told him of their plans to move to the country which were being held up by their lack of funds. Asked how much they needed David mentioned the figure of £3,000. To his amazement the visitor said he could provide them with that sum. Since that time this businessman had taken a special interest in the commune's search for a rural home. During my stay at the community I accompanied David to the Bond Street offices of the businessman where he was to receive the news about their latest attempt to purchase property. The idea was that the businessman was to buy the property for himself, and then let it to the community on a ten year, rent-free lease with a further option at the end of that period. The upland farm they had been hoping to buy was in Cornwall, but once again the story was that someone else was prepared to pay more for the property than was the businessman. This delay naturally caused fears to grow with David that eventually the businessman would decide to buy whichever farm took his fancy without considering the special needs and wishes of the community. This of course is always the risk when you depend on someone else for financial support. You are to an extent in the hands of that person or institution.

Apart from the farm in the country, David also anticipated that since the community had attained the status of a housing association there should eventually be a whole variety of community houses working in co-operation together. As part of this long-term development he anticipated that the community would establish an emergency housing scheme in Chiswick in the not-too-distant future where people like Pat could have a roof over their heads.

The ability of the community to expand its ventures in this way would obviously have been impossible without the links that had been established with outside bodies and people. These links had been established at least in part because the work that the community was doing was so readily recognisable by outsiders as 'worthwhile'. To the public David could point to the 'successes' of the community: to the addicts that had kicked their habit whilst living in the community, to the drifters who had found and kept a job, to the social isolates who had formed lasting and stable relationships with others through living in the community. In fact his own personal definition of a success for the community was when, through living in the community, an individual developed the strength and commitment to live a life in which they cared for others, when they realised the richness of a life led caring for others as one would for one's brothers and sisters. Whatever his personal definition of a success, the public definition of the 'good works' done by the community in restoring deviants to the straight and narrow path of conventionality had resulted in the slow and gradual development of good relationships with the various public agencies of social control such as the police and the social workers who can make life so difficult for communities if they choose.

Thus, although the community had a reputation in the immediate neighbourhood as a centre of drugs and hippies, without causing much concern to the members of the community, good relations had slowly developed with the local police. These relationships developed gradually through the police repeatedly having to come to collect someone from the community for some offence or other, and through this contact realising that the community was something more than a haven for petty criminals and junkies, that it was an attempt by some committed people to achieve something 'worthwhile'. Whilst relations were especially good with the uniformed branch of the local police, I was informed that some of the plain-clothes CID men could be a bit sticky. However, as an illustration of their 'understanding' with the police, one girl told me of the time when the police had received orders to raid the community for drugs. They turned up, following their orders and searched the house and, sure enough, they found illegal drugs on the premises. However, they reported back to their superiors that they had found no drugs there. Another illustration was provided in conversation with the policeman who had come to take the particulars of John, the junkie who died whilst I was at the community. In between refusing offers of food and coffee from the commune members he told us that when he was off duty and met someone who seemed in need of a roof over their heads and a home, then he frequently referred them to the community. Having a Justice of the Peace on their support group had not done any harm to the public image of the community either. The members laughingly talked about the frequency of David's appearances in court to speak on behalf of one or other of the members and how it seemed that he only had to appear and a lenient sentence was passed on the defendant.

Over time good relationships had also developed with local social work agencies such as the probation service and, in particular, 'New Horizons', an experimental social work agency established in Soho that tried to provide an advisory service to the young drifters and junkies of Soho and the West End. Such agencies frequently referred people with whom they came into contact to the community. Such contacts were furthered through people from the community, almost inevitably David, going out to speak to groups such as student Community Action societies about the activities and aims of the group. Invariably such addresses would end with an open invitation to the audience to come along to the community any day for the six o'clock evening meal when they could meet the other members.

Despite such close links that had been established with outside bodies and individuals, virtually no contact had been made with the Commune Movement. David echoed the feelings of other commune members that the Commune Movement as such was 'an amorphous and possibly meaningless body'.

Internal organisation

That links with the Commune Movement and other communes were very slight and tenuous can be attributed in part to the essential differences between Kingsway and other communities. One member explained it as follows: 'In a way the people living here have not consciously chosen to do so except the house workers. People have ended up here.'[3] What this means is that with other communes people have, whilst following the path to community, made a conscious choice for themselves that they would like to live in a commune and have then found one in which to live in preference to a variety of alternative courses of action. For many of the members at Kingsway such alternative courses of action have not been available—they are people to whom things are done rather than people who are aware of their freedom of choice and action. They are people who have been processed through social work agencies, through prisons and mental hospitals, and who have 'ended up' at Kingsway because they had no other place to go. For many when they first arrive at the community it represents the least unattractive option open to them rather than the attainment of some searched-for goal that such a moment often represents to people who join other communal groups. Given the fact that many of the members of the community have developed, by the time they arrive, certain characteristics and habits which makes it very difficult for them to operate adequately in straight society—whether this be a violent temper, a drug habit, or an inability to communicate meaningfully with others—then one would expect that with such a variety of 'maladjusted' (to use a horrible and disgusting label) people living together in close quarters, an orderly existence would be made virtually impossible without some set of commonly agreed-upon rules and regulations for directing everyday activity.

In fact at Kingsway there were rules, but with one or two exceptions these were more in the nature of guidelines for action rather than firmly laid-down orders which a person ignored at his peril. Of course, if such rules were resorted to it would defeat one of the prime objects of the community, to establish an extended family environment, an alternative to what David described as 'that cramping and crushing little affair sometimes called the nuclear family'. The existence of strictly laid-down rules and regulations would constitute the complete negation of the guiding beliefs of the community—the determination to 'deal with each other as brothers and sisters . . . not because it is to our personal advantage, not because we will get something out of it, but simply as we have life in us.'

What rules there were, such as those laid down in the agreement quoted above, were guided by two major principles. On the one hand there were those made for the sake of the health and safety of individuals and members in general. Thus, any registered addict was formally required to hand over his supply to a houseworker who kept the supply in the house safe and distributed the drugs according to the individual addict's prescription. Apart from a concern to guard against drug abuse this rule had been made with a view to the consequences that could occur if a small child found some barbiturates or some other drug lying around the house and ate them. Thus, any drugs that were found around the house were destroyed. The other rules had been decided upon in order to promote the values of co-operation between the members. Such rules were more in the nature of 'expectations' held of the 'ideal member' and only the repeated transgression of these expectations, particularly the expectation about appearance at the evening meal, would cause the offender to receive a word in his or her ear from one of the other members.

The guidelines along which the affairs of the community were run reflect the original principles which inspired David to embark on the venture, and whilst all rules and decisions were formally agreed upon by a house meeting which all members were expected to attend, in practice much of the initiative in raising issues and questions to be decided upon came from David, usually after some preliminary discussion with other long-term members of the community. The house meetings themselves occurred fairly frequently, and could take place during the course of the evening meal or else as a 'special event' on a Sunday. Issues that might be raised ranged from the problem of what to do about a particular member who was refusing to make any financial contribution to the house, to how to manage necessary repair work upon the property, how to organise a system of volunteers to man the local shop run by the Society for the Blind, how long they would be willing to provide accommodation for a visiting sociologist, and so on. The house meeting was also important as an occasion when David could inform the other members of the latest developments in their long search for a farm and other matters of common concern.

When I first visited the community in 1970 David told me of how he had resigned his post as an art teacher in a local comprehensive school due to the pressures of his life in the community. By 1972 his range of activities had not changed much. His time was spent on administrative matters, answering letters and such like, stopping fights, lending a sympathetic ear to those with particular problems, acting as an agent for those members in search of jobs, accommodation or whatever. Visiting social work agencies and also members or friends of the community who were in hospital or prison also took up a significant proportion of his time.

Although the agreement of the community required everyone 'to take their part in preparing the meals, in clearing and cleaning and maintaining their house, personal and common areas alike', in practice many of the members took little part in such activities. Much of the food consumed by the members of the community consisted of perishable goods provided free of charge by a local store which had been approached by the chairman of the support group. One member in particular, a young ex-mental hospital patient, had begun to take a special interest in preparing the evening meal, whilst another member, a young but long-term girl member, went out each morning to buy the standard daily shopping items such as tea and sugar. Apart from this division of labour, a number of members took little or no part in preparing meals, washing up, or generally keeping the house clean and tidy. This situation reflected the attitude of certain members who went out to work each day. From their wages they paid a weekly sum into the communal purse and then felt that they had done their bit for the community. Their attitude was 'Why should we work around the house when we are going out to work each day and paying our share of the costs when other members are not?' This tendency to treat the community as little more than a lodging house or hotel was one of the major problems experienced by some of the more committed members. A regular sight in the mornings at Kingsway was that of people coming down from their rooms to get themselves some breakfast and then returning to their rooms while Brian the house worker and one or two others would be busying themselves cleaning and tidying. A number of members who were not working outside the community seemed to spend a large proportion of their time in their rooms. However, no attempt was made to formalise any system of allotting tasks to people—chores like washing up and so on were done on an *ad hoc* basis according to whoever happened to be around and felt the urge to help out.

Amongst those who were not engaged in full-time employment outside the community, a limited number spent a proportion of their day working in the garage which the community had converted into a small workshop with the aid of a grant of money from the Nuffield Foundation. Here the community made simple puzzles for children of two years and upwards. They also made hobby horses, rag dolls and nursery cushions. In October 1972 they were waiting for word from the Design Centre, to whom they had sent samples of their work, about possible outlets and orders for their work.

Most members spent their time after the evening meal either sitting around talking or watching the television in the common room, or else would be upstairs in their rooms or out and about their business. One evening a week all those who felt like it would go over to the church hall across the road to play table tennis. One evening a week used to be spent by some of the members doing clay modelling, but this had just ceased when I arrived as the 'classes' had been held by two women teachers from outside, and as one of them could no longer spare the time the other had felt unable to continue alone. Apart from these activities, there was also a weekly 'house activity', when all who felt like it went out as a group to the cinema or perhaps to watch David perform in his capacity as an amateur boxer. It was explained to me that this weekly group venture was important in that for many of the members the only times they went out anywhere was either to the pub or else up to the 'Dilly to 'score'.

Finances

As has been said, the house itself was not owned by the community, but was rented. By 1972 it was estimated that the weekly cost of running the house, paying the rent, rates, fuel bills and purchasing food came to around £60 a week. The rent was £40 a month. This sum was raised largely by members paying a weekly amount, usually about £6 for those in full-time employment, into the communal purse. Ideally, it was hoped that people who worked outside would put all their money into the pool, but in fact they tended to put in what they felt they could afford. People on supplementary benefits and other forms of state assistance also contributed what they felt they could afford. Repeated failure to pay any rent when it was known that a person had the necessary funds was generally made a matter for discussion at the house meetings. David and Brian, the two houseworkers, drew what they needed from the petty cash, which in fact was usually taken care of by David. In addition to such sources of revenue, a limited amount was derived from the sale of the produce from the craft workshop. The community also received donations from individuals and charitable bodies such as the Nuffield Foundation which enabled it to save the sum of about £3,000, mainly with a view to providing the necessary capital that would be required to equip themselves when they moved to the farm.

Problems and future prospects

Since the bulk of the members of the Kingsway Community have 'ended up there' as opposed to having consciously chosen freely to live communally from a whole range of other options, the problems confronted by the people living there differ in some degree from the problems confronting other communards. All the members shared the problem of having to live in close proximity to others whose companionship was not freely chosen. They were to a certain extent forced to interact with people amongst whom, to put it simply, there were those they did not like. Obviously, for many of those who had been directed to the community by social workers and such like, those who appeared for some reason or other to be 'socially inadequate', their major problem as individuals remained that of coping with the world—the problem of managing their drug addiction, the problem of communicating with others, the problem of controlling their violent and aggressive natures, the general problem of getting rid of their accustomed habits and tendencies, always assuming that they wished to transcend their customary ways of thinking, acting and relating to others.

For those members who had come to share David's philosophy about the richness of a life led caring for others as one would care for the members of one's own immediate family, a major problem involved the difficulties confronted in trying to get others to view the community in a similar light. As has been mentioned, there were those members of the community who worked outside in full-time employment who viewed the project merely as a lodging house or private hotel; there were the addicts whose sole concern was to score sufficient junk to satisfy their habits; and there were others who appeared to make no attempt whatsoever to communicate with the other members and seemingly refused to participate in the life of the community except at the minimal level of occasionally turning up for the evening meal. All members, however, shared the problem of over-crowding which had plagued the community on occasions during its life. It was interesting to discover, however, that it was not so much the actual numbers in residence which determined whether or not people felt the house to be too crowded for ease and comfort. Rather, it was influenced very much by the state of morale within the community as a whole. That is, during my visit in 1972 there was the feeling within the community that the house was strong, that people were together, that the situation within the community had stabilised and strengthened after a period of flux and rapid turnover of members, and so on. Thus, although this state of affairs could be partly attributable to the actual decrease in membership numbers, there was an increased willingness on the part of the community members to accept new members who were in need of a warm and caring environment such as could be found at Kingsway because, it was felt, the house could take it. Conceivably this feeling could well lead to an increase in numbers until such time as the feeling grew that the people in the community were no longer together, that they were no longer strong, and that they could no longer spare the energies required to care for new and additional members. Then there would be a slow decline in numbers until the feeling of strength and the desire to help other outsiders grew once more. One would therefore expect that the size of membership of the Kingsway Community would show a cyclical nature, a time of growth followed by one of decline followed by a period of renewed growth.

However, the future undoubtedly held further expansions in store for the community. It was anticipated that as a housing association the community would build in the Chiswick area of London in the not-too-distant future a centre providing emergency accommodation for the homeless of that area. In addition, of course, there was the farm. In some ways it had been the prospect of the farm that had held a small group of long-term community members together over the years. There was the feeling amongst them in October 1972 of 'we only have to last out until Christmas and then we shall be off to the country'. Of course they had had their hopes dashed before, but one would imagine that this experience of having one's hopes repeatedly destroyed can only be borne for so long before people start to lose hope and faith and begin to drift off along other channels. This would then mean that when the farm finally was obtained, David and the remainder would be faced with the problem of gathering together a new solid core-group of committed members to form the back-bone of the rural project. Problems could also arise if, through their desperation to obtain property, they unwittingly placed themselves in the hands of some benefactor who insisted upon having a determining voice in any decisions made concerning the new community. The existing members depended a great deal upon David as the leader of the group, as the person who could be relied upon—the rock. This was his role, whether he liked it or not. The consequences for Kingsway of David's departure to the rural venture could prove very problematic unless others appeared who could at least take over some of his duties.

Until such time as they did move out into the country David and the other committed members would have to continue to cope with the problems of over-crowding (most members, including David, shared a room with two or three others), the occasional eruptions of violence and conflict,[4] the disappointments of seeing members who seemed to be making progress revert to their old ways of drug abuse, alcoholism or whatever, and the general wear and tear on one's physical and mental strength that accompanies living a life in which one's time is almost totally taken up with caring for others without having sufficient time to devote to one's own development and welfare. Despite these problems, living at Kingsway had its rewards for those who had consciously chosen to live there. Primarily there was the enjoyment of the richness, as they saw it, of a life led within a community in which people care for each other. In addition there was the future hope of community houses springing up around the country, all working together in co-operation. Against the occasional feelings of despair with the slow and difficult task of convincing people that a community has so much to offer to people, there was the vision of a slow-burning domestic revolution that was taking place and which they were promoting. The following was written by a member towards the end of 1971 and it expresses these feelings perfectly :[5]

> Our home is very shabby and ill-equipped but we provide the tolerance and care necessary for a person to gain relief from distress and bitterness. We know that for many of our guests to be truly valued as a person is the most important thing of all.
>
> There is a friendliness and tolerance in the Kingsway Community too often lacking in our society. Yet it would be foolish to overlook its great problems. Deep psychological

damage is not easily healed. Often time and patience is required. But we have found that people always respond to an opportunity to share their lives and their problems in an atmosphere of love and concern. In the seven years in which the Community has been functioning many have gained a new lease of life. The time is now ripe for our community to enlarge its horizons and for other communities to be set up on similar lines. The first need is for people to come by choice to join with us. No community where many people have grave problems can function at its full potential without members able to give consistent and strong support. It is just such inter-action of people at various levels of need and development which makes for maturity and for a whole society.

To join us would involve some sacrifices. Rather uncomfortable conditions plus the general difficulties of communal living with some people who are disturbed. Yet those who could be of real value will not be put off by such things. For they must have reached a level of development at which it is realised that to live fully and happily oneself it is essential to love and serve other people; and that to be concerned solely about one's own welfare is a most dreadful form of slavery.

The aim of these communities is nothing short of revolution. Not a violent revolution which by its very nature makes no difference; but a basic change in human consciousness. We wish to help produce a society in which people really know that they are members one of another and must therefore be vitally concerned about the welfare of every human being.

This may sound somewhat grandiose. We know how small and apparently insignificant we are at the moment. Yet often big powerful movements blow themselves to pieces whereas the small seemingly powerless ones have most lasting effect.

Our ideas and values are certainly not new. They originated at least 2,000 years ago with the early Christians who were the original and the true communists. All the faithful, we are told, held together, sharing all they had as each had need.

Yet today ideals are more important than ever. We live in a world which we are in danger of destroying if we continue in a self-centred existence. It is growing even bigger and more complex. Thousands of people live in bed-sitting rooms;

possibly millions in limited, narrow family groups largely alienated from their neighbours. In these circumstances the need to re-establish community is vital.

Whether this revolution in consciousness succeeds does not depend merely on historical necessity: it depends on you. It can only happen when sufficient people understand and desire it.

Chapter 5

Postlip Hall: a practical commune

'A way of having your semi and your jam as well.'

Origins and beliefs

I travelled to Postlip Hall, a Jacobean mansion sited in the Cotswolds amidst beautiful English scenery, through Oxfordshire from London. In London I had spent some time with a friend who had also visited Postlip taking photographs. He told me of the 'bloody amazing' house he had encountered, of its grounds and of the beauty of the hills around. I myself approached the community with my usual feeling of trepidation tempered with a certain confidence that came from the surrounding scenery. It was a beautiful autumn day and I thought as I drove up to the house, 'What the hell if they do turn out to be shit people, when there is scenery like this to enjoy.'

In fact the members of the community at Postlip, if community it can be called, turned out to be pleasant and much like I had expected. Although I had never visited the group before I knew something of its history through articles that had appeared about it in the national press. I knew that Postlip differed from other communal groups in that the prime motives behind the establishment of the venture were practical ones rather than idealistic aspirations about changing the world and creating a new alternative society. Two of the founding families had first come together whilst living a few miles apart in Gloucestershire, having realised how much money could be saved through buying groceries in bulk from a wholesaler. From this first enterprise in practical co-operation to save money the grander venture had grown, guided by similar ideas.

It would be wrong to say that the only motives behind the members of Postlip coming together into a communal venture were practical ones—the anticipated benefits of sharing the costs of running a large house with others, the advantages of bulk buying groceries, the prospect of having others around to look after one's children and baby-sit, etc. These were the prime motives for most of the members, but there were others. Thus, one of their number wrote:[1]

> We are a loose gestalt of powerful individualists who chance at this point to be moving in roughly the same direction, and who like travelling together. Spin-offs are partly practical, like bulk-buying for hungry kids—cats—passing Irishmen, a shared second car (that word 'second' marks us off, doesn't it?), and a fantastically mind-stretching environment for—in our terms—buttons; and partly the feeling that little boxes are not for living. No, that's not it, either.
>
> Maybe it's diversity: the chance to buck a chain-saw in the morning, de-shit an old and recalcitrant boiler and plant bulbs in the afternoon, pick apples in the late p.m.; and read poetry aloud in the evening around the fire, with beer and people and talk. . . . But Postlip is a deliberate attempt to construct an improvement on little boxes for us and for the children.

Membership and recruitment

Postlip, for its members, represented what one of them phrased, 'a way of having your semi and your jam as well'. Sited in fourteen-and-a-half acres of land, the Hall was purchased by the group for £20,000 in the summer of 1970, the mortgage being provided to what was by then the Postlip Housing Association by their local authority. In addition to the original purchase price the housing association had to raise an additional £22,000 to convert the hall into four self-contained living units and two smaller cottages at the rear of the main structure. With the exception of one large room, all the living space was 'private'. Each living unit housed a separate family which had nine or ten rooms for its private use. The cottages only had about six rooms. In late 1972 one of them housed the only unmarried member of the community, a twenty-six-year-old educational psychologist, whilst the other was the weekend and holiday home of a family who spent the week in London, the husband working as a senior educational psychologist with the London Education Authority and the wife as an architect. The other adult members, eight in number, were all drawn from a similar middle-class social group. Sandy was an officer in the RAF who in 1972 was working as a lecturer with Rolls Royce at Bristol and his wife Jan trained as a painter at the Slade School of Art. Chris was a civil engineer with a firm at Stratford and his wife, Jay, spent her time writing novels, although without any great commercial success. Ian was a local GP and his wife, Jane, had been a life-long friend of Jan whom she met whilst at the Slade. John, at fifty-six the eldest member of the community, was a businessman who had suffered a number of heart attacks which brought about his early retirement. His wife, Helen, was an accomplished violinist. In addition to these adults, the Hall was home for ten kids aged between three and eleven.

As was mentioned above, the origins of the community can be traced to the period when two of the families began participating together in a food co-operative venture in Gloucestershire. From there the idea grew of purchasing a large property with lots of space which would provide them with a much nicer living environment than they could possibly afford as individual and separate purchasing units. Ian and Jane, as friends of one of the original couples, were invited to join the scheme and when the property at Postlip was finally found they moved from Colchester to join. The couple who had maintained their jobs and house in the Home Counties joined in response to an advert in the press. The eldest couple, John and Helen, came after having their enthusiasm aroused by a rather critical article on the group that appeared in the *Sunday Telegraph*. The process by which they came to join the venture gives one some idea of the way in which Postlip copes with the problem of recruitment.

John and his wife had been living in the south of England. He had retired from a senior executive business position following a heart attack. They wanted to move from the area and when they saw the article in the *Sunday Telegraph* they thought that Postlip might be the place for them. They rang the community and arranged a visit. They came for a day during which they went from one family

G

to the next, being 'sized up' by the existing members and forming their own impressions about the place. In John's words, it was all 'very polite and very proper'. They stayed the night, and during the course of the evening it was intimated to them that they would be very welcome to make their home there if they so wished.

During the early period of life at the community the members were very open to the national press and articles on the venture appeared in such papers as *New Society*, *Vanity Fair*, and the *Sunday Times* as well as the *Sunday Telegraph*, and the local press. This concern to spread the news of their project abroad was part of a conscious attempt to recruit new members and to convince them that Postlip was a viable and thriving venture. They also advertised in personal columns for new members. In fact, they saw about 100 people who came to Postlip with a view to joining before choosing the final two families. Given this number of potential recruits I was surprised to hear that they had in fact only given a definite refusal to two families out of this number. The rest had all decided for themselves that Postlip was not the place for them.

In fact this experience of the members at Postlip mirrored very closely that of another communal group with which I had established contact some time previously. Like Postlip, the nucleus of committed communards were middle-aged people pursuing middle-class professions of one sort or another. Unlike Postlip, however, they did not possess any property but were involved in a search for some. The saga of their attempts to form a commune is captured in the following quote from a letter I received from one of their number:

> I would like you to know that after 3 years, Michael's venture is so far a complete failure. When he has the people he has not the house, and when he has the house he has not the people, and never has he had enough money. . . . We had one lovely house, and at the very last moment three people fell out (both out of the project and with one another).

For this venture recruits with sufficient capital to help purchase a substantial piece of property were needed. Postlip required the same sort of people: those who could afford to make the required substantial financial deposit in the Housing Association and also afford to pay a fairly substantial 'rent' to the Housing Association to enable it to repay the mortgage. Those who can afford to make such financial investments are exactly those who have most to lose by dropping out of the conventional world. They are those who are likely to have fairly well-paid jobs. They are also likely to have their own private homes which they would have to sell in order to raise the necessary capital. On moving to their new home they would also be faced with the problem of finding employment similar in kind and in financial reward to that which they had previously enjoyed. They are also likely to feel a responsibility for the care and protection of their spouses and their children. For such people, the really big step is that which must be taken from the stage of being 'interested' in communal living to that of actually putting that interest into practice. When faced with having to make the decision —the choice of whether to risk giving up the way of life one has become used to over the years for a new way of life with new people about which and about whom one's knowledge is limited, or whether to take the safe course of sticking to the devil that one knows—then in the majority of cases the decision is to refrain from making the final step. It is a much easier matter for a young, unattached and poverty-stricken person to change the course of his life by joining a commune than it is for those who have travelled a fair way along the path of a normal existence and in the process acquired customary habits of living and felt responsibilities to family and kin. It was for this reason that the original members of Postlip had sought, through the mass media, to convince potential members that theirs was a practical and viable venture which could offer to the recruit a richer and more rewarding life than was possible in a suburban semi.

In fact, in the two and a quarter years of its existence since 1970 Postlip had only lost one member. This was a single person. He was younger than the rest of the members. He was a homosexual and, according to one of the members, had real problems of identity—he didn't know what he wanted or where he was going. He had found it difficult to relate to the other members and with time this difficulty increased. Gradually he became more and more of a 'loner' until eventually he decided to leave. As a housing association the community had a legal structure which provided the formal rules for people leaving and joining the group. When they joined people became co-owners of the property through investing money into the Association which then 'leased' them living space. These rules also allowed for a person who wished to leave to sell up, take their money and go, just as with any private property transaction.

Relations with outside

One of the consequences of Postlip advertising its existence to the outside world was that apart from attracting potential members, such publicity also attracted visitors in their hordes. One of the members, concluding an article written for *Communes*, provided the address of the community and invited people to visit them, although for preference having contacted them beforehand. The result of this was that the group were visited by some of the hundreds of young people who, estranged from the existing order of things, were looking for an alternative way of life for themselves. I had assumed that this would have brought a number of hassles for the members of the group. In fact they told me they enjoyed the visits of the 'long haired weirdoes' although the members of the group are in a marginal kind of position with regard to the 'underground', just as they are in a marginal position with regard to straight society.[2]

Along with members of other practical communes the members of Postlip occupy a rather peculiar position. On the one hand the men amongst them, at least, pursued straight occupations in the world outside. On the other hand they were experimenting with living arrangements which are significantly different from those pursued by the bulk of their contemporaries. On the one hand they feel a great deal of sympathy with the aims and aspirations of the younger, more idealistic people involved with communes; on the other hand they feel themselves to be somewhat apart from them in that they are more affluent, older, and more 'bourgeois' in their attitudes and style of life than other communards. The members of Postlip were set in their middle-class ways and styles of family life before they came to form a communal venture, and much of these remained. This peculiar position was expressed in the article already quoted:[3]

> At first sight—or even second—we don't have two ideals to scratch together, which is a gulf between us and the movement. And we're rather older and more battered, which is another . . . we are a good deal too middle-class for most of your readers. . . . We are also prepared to make accommodations and compromises with the totally square world so as to arrange the space and life-style which we now think we want. To make Postlip happen, we had to do a good deal of tie-wearing, and make some very

middle-class noises in the direction of our local Rural District
Council, who are financing the project. . . . You will see that we
are very much on the fringe of the Commune Movement. For one
thing, without being unkind or snotty, we have rather more money
and are consequently able to go more deeply into debt to create
this fairly square but ambitious construct. For another, we're
not mystical, nor do we have a unifying and deeply-felt principle.
. . . You might say that we are poised between the entirely
straight world, much of which we dislike and reject; and the total
commitment to communality which most of your members feel.
This could be a very uneasy and uncomfortable position, but we
don't find it so. We have retained enough of our middle-class
approaches to want private houses within the gestalt of Postlip;
but discarded enough of them to want Postlip, and to work to
make it happen.

Despite the awareness of their rather marginal position with
regard to other communal ventures, the members at Postlip were
keen to help other ventures with practical advice on such matters as
how to form a housing association and the like. They had also
established links with other projects. Thus they had personal
contact with the Taena Community which is one of the few remaining groups that were formed immediately prior to World War
Two by pacifists in Britain, and which is sited in the Cotswolds.[4]
They had also acted as week-end hosts to a group who were seeking
to form a commune in the south-west of England, and had sought
to help and advise a group who had moved to the south-west of
Scotland to form a commune. The property for this group was
purchased with the aid of £25,000 earned from an architecture
commission obtained by one of their number, and from the sale of
members' private homes. This communal venture appeared, to the
members at Postlip, to be doomed to failure. The members were
from similar social backgrounds to the Postlip dwellers, but they
were seeking to establish a much more communal kind of living
experiment than the people at Postlip felt they themselves could
manage. The problems and tensions that were being experienced at
the Scottish community were a direct result, they felt, of an attempt
to share financial resources, eating and living space, and household
tasks amongst all the members of the community, without sufficient
thought for the consequences of such arrangements for individuals

accustomed to nuclear family life with its privacy and separation between people.

Whilst the community had good relations with other experiments in communal living, their relationships with their immediate neighbours were not so good. The previous owner of the Hall lived in a lodge in the grounds and, according to the community dwellers, regretted the low price for which she sold the property when, across the valley, a similar property, although modernised, had been sold in the autumn of 1972 to Tony Jacklin, the golfer, for over £100,000. The result was that there was some bitterness on her part towards the occupants of her former home. However, they persisted in their efforts to establish cordial relations with her. Their only other immediate neighbours were the occupants of the farms surrounding their land. Relations with these appeared to be reasonable, although they threatened to sue one who emptied a tank of creosote into the stream that ran through their land and poisoned their fish. He in turn threatened to shoot their dogs for bothering his sheep. The result was that whilst ten children can be found around the community, the visitor searched in vain for a friendly dog. However, the Hall itself is sited a couple of miles outside the local village of Winchcombe, and to get to the house you have to make your way up a drive that must be three-quarters of a mile long—hardly the kind of situation that facilitates neighbours just 'dropping in as they were passing'. The result of this was that the contact between the village and the commune dwellers was limited to them doing their shopping and drinking in the village whilst the children also went to local schools. They did not make any attempt to proselytise about their way of life to their neighbours in any way whatsoever, and their purely social links with villagers were limited.

Certain of the members did involve themselves with a regional group for the advancement of state education (CASE), although this involvement had ceased by 1972. However, by the autumn of 1972, with the major structural alterations to the living areas of the Hall having been completed, they were beginning to turn their attentions to future projects and plans. Amongst these was the idea of converting the ancient Tithe Barn in the grounds into an arts centre, a place where people in the Cotswolds could come to listen to music or to look at painting exhibitions and the like. They had already held a concert which had been a great success in terms of the numbers of people who had turned up, whilst they had also held an exhibition of paintings as a result of which two painters in the community managed to sell some of their work. Apart from being an anticipated source of finance, this venture was seen by at least some of the members as an example of Postlip getting involved with the local social scene, providing a service for lovers of music and art in general living in the Cotswolds and Gloucestershire.

Internal organisation

The barn had been cleaned out and made ready for the anticipated concerts and exhibitions largely by the men of the community at the week-ends and in their spare time. During the week all the men, except John, went out to work whilst the women stayed at home looking after their pre-school age children, if they had any of that age, and getting on with their own artistic pursuits. The household units were completely separate from each other, each had its own lockable front door, and within them each family looked after itself in exactly the same manner as in any middle-class home—meals were taken separately in family groups, each unit had its own kitchen. Household tasks were not shared but each family was responsible for its own private living space. There were no formal rules dictating how life should be organised within the separate family units, neither were there any formal rules governing interaction between members in the community as a whole.

No person was recognised as a leader at Postlip, each member tending to emphasise his own individuality and his desire to hang on to it. Although there were no leaders, naturally enough certain people had particular skills and capabilities which meant that they developed a special responsibility for particular areas of life at the Hall. Thus, Chris was a civil engineer and it seemed natural that he should be the member who took the major interest in supervising the conversion work done on the building. He was the one who examined the various tenders, sent off the queries and dealt with the correspondence. John, brought up in an Anglo-Irish landed family and with a lifetime's experience of meeting and dealing with people acted as the community's public relations man whenever it became a matter of dealing with local government officials and the like. Sandy, an ex-RAF officer, was a very capable administrator and tended to look after the routine administrative matters that needed to be seen to. He had also had a long-term interest in hydroponics.[5] Ian had taken a special interest in one of the new ventures at Postlip, the trout farming. It was decided that it would be an enjoyable and ultimately profitable project to utilise the streams and the ponds in their grounds by developing some sort of fish farm. They cleaned up the waters and purchased their first generation of trout. Despite the fact that they had lost all their fish through the carelessness of one of the local farmers who poisoned the river, during my visit I was shown the 2,000 or so young trout that were being reared and which were destined, eventually, to be sold for stocking lakes and rivers. Ian had also taken a special interest in what was hoped would be another of Postlip's future projects, the growing of grapes for wine making and for eating. The land itself was recognised as belonging to all the members of the community and whilst care of the lawns was considered to be everyone's responsibility, if someone wanted to develop a vegetable patch, such as Chris had done, then he could just go along to that area of land which had been used for growing vegetables in the past and start clearing up his patch. In other words, there was no communal vegetable patch. Chris had grown vegetables in 1972 and these he sold to the other members of the community. Ian and Jane had started to grow some but they let the weeds take over and eventually lost their plants in the jungle of weeds that grew. Unlike the members of the commune in Norfolk, the members did use weed-killers and chemicals on the garden. They claimed, however, that they were very aware of the dangers of pollution and sought only to use those chemical aids the effects of which they felt they could control.

In addition to having these special areas of interest, the men had all worked together clearing up the waste and overgrown land around the place. The fact that the other male members were working hard on this whilst he was away in London was not lost on the psychologist. As a result he presented the community with a motorised machine for clearing land—this was his contribution to the joint effort. It was emphasised to me that this had not been asked for by the other members of the group, but had been made of his own free will as a gift. At the same time one gained the distinct impression that the donor had set himself a precedent for the future where labour on a communal project was unevenly divided between the members.

These various projects had all been developed in the period since the community began in 1970. It was felt by the members that some organisational framework was necessary to cope with these new ventures and the solution they finally came up with was the Postlip Society. This Society was organised like any other formed by people with an interest in common such as bird-watchers or whatever. Membership fees were charged but it was open to people outside the community, although the rules were such as to ensure that the determining voice on all matters of policy rested with members of the community. The Society would be able to raise loans to finance its ventures, and one of the community members had guaranteed one bank loan of £1,000. It was the Society that organised and financed the events that took place in the Tithe Barn and it was to the Society that any profits made on such occasions would accrue. The Society also had executive officers. For instance, Jan was the treasurer, and other members held the other positions.

The Society 'leased' the barn from the Housing Association which also had its own formal structure. All the adult members were directors of the Association, with John as the chairman and Ian as the treasurer. By law the Association was required to hold annual general meetings at which minutes were kept. As the property was divided up into four large units along with two cottages which were considered half-units, formal voting power within the Association was allocated accordingly. Thus, each full unit had two votes, each cottage or half-unit had one vote. In practice any adult member could exert a kind of veto power against any policy question with which they disagreed.

Apart from such formal arrangements required by the law, there was little sign at Postlip of any other attempts to establish formalised rules and procedures for coping with issues. Decisions and new ventures tended to emerge as a result of an informal system of people going round the community 'sounding out' the other members about their opinions on the matter in question. Likewise, they had no formalised or regular method for coping with the tensions that developed between members as inevitably happens from time to time in any community. In fact, this matter of how to cope with inter-personal problems was a matter of some argument and disagreement within the community. The method of coping with tension between members was for them to adopt the typical middle-class procedure of withdrawing to their own living area and there fume about the other person until one felt able to resume once again the façade necessary for polite and proper intercourse. In other words, no attempt was made to confront issues of personal disagreement and interpersonal tension. They were papered over and left to lie dormant beneath the surface. This was the way the members had been accustomed to acting in their middle-class lives prior to joining the group, and they drew back from any temptation to be open and completely honest with each other about their feelings —for that would be rudeness and might lead to unpleasantness and, after all, one just does not go round intentionally hurting others' feelings by telling them what you *really* feel about them. The two psychologists amongst them, however, felt that they should try and be open with each other, they should be honest about their feelings for other members, they should confront the people they disliked with their criticism of them, and thereby bring everything out onto the surface and be forced to resolve the differences in an honest and open fashion. The other members, however, steadfastly refused to listen to the pleas of the psychologists and preferred to harbour their grievances within the walls of their own private living space.

Thus, amongst some of the members there was a feeling that Chris was not only inconsiderate in his treatment of the other people, he was also paranoid, believing that others were scheming against him. Of course, in fact, they *were* scheming against him in so far as they talked about him and his latest inconsiderate exploits behind his back in the privacy of their flats. By failing to confront Chris with their criticisms of his behaviour, such as his habit of inviting people to visit him and then going out for the day having forgotten all about his guests and so leaving the other members to cope with them, they were only contributing to what Lemert has termed the 'dynamics of paranoia' and perpetuating what was basically a fundamental dishonesty in their dealings with each other.[6] The result was that whilst they remained true to their middle-class norms about not offending people by criticising them to their face, they also ensured that the interpersonal tensions remained un-resolved, to 'fester' under the surface of polite interaction. Now whilst this strategy might work in a middle-class housing estate where you can consciously avoid meeting those whom you dislike, in a community where you are almost forced to interact with each other this strategy would seem almost inevitably to lead up an ever-increasing spiral of tension, that can only be broken either by bringing it all out into the open and facing up to the differences or by one of the parties leaving the group, which seemed more likely in the case of Postlip.[7]

Although like other communal groups Postlip did not have formal rules and regulations, they did have 'ways of doing things' and conventions which were not written down. These ranged from where to park your car to the generally accepted custom that if you went into the village for the Sunday papers you got everyone else's papers at the same time. You also knocked before entering someone else's living area. You did not interfere with another family's domestic troubles. If you spent an evening round at another's flat and they remarked that it was getting late, you took the hint and your leave. In other words, just as life in a block of flats is not necessarily ruled by a whole series of regulations but life goes on in an orderly enough fashion because neighbours come to understandings about things, so life at Postlip ticked over because the members shared a common set of understandings about what was right and proper for what kinds of situations. And, of course, much of the tension that occurred between people arose through one of them perceiving that the other had transgressed these often unarticulated understandings.

How did the new member learn these unwritten rules and customs? Like any stranger entering a new social group it could take time to learn the accepted ways of going about things, but basically one had to acquire as much knowledge of them as one could through paying attention to what others did and through listening to the advice of the others. In this process John played a particularly important role. As the oldest member in terms of age he was to a certain extent allotted the 'father-figure' role. He was allowed the freedom denied others to interfere in other people's affairs. The fact that he had taken on the role of smoothing troubled waters was also attributable to the fact that he was the only male who was not engaged in full-time employment outside the community, and so had more time to spend on 'human relations' within the group. The sort of thing that could happen would be for John to come across Sandy muttering to himself in a bad-tempered fashion. John would find out from him that the cause of this anguish was that the new member had parked his car again in Sandy's accustomed spot. Old John would then wander round to the new member's living area and in conversation happen to mention that Sandy was a bit upset because the new member was taking up his parking spot—'you could park there if you wanted but why not park it in such and such a place, it will make no difference for you and Sandy would probably appreciate it' would be how the conversation would ensue. The new member had learnt a new rule. The new member could also look through the diary that used to be kept in the one room that was treated as a communal area in order to gain some understanding about how things were done at Postlip. This book was to be used by anyone who felt like writing in it what he had done that day, what they happened to have felt and thought, what had upset them that day, what plans they had for the future and so on. It was hoped that this diary would provide an important means of communication between the members. Also, it had been discovered that so many things were going on within the community, that people lost track of time and dates etc., and so it was expected that the diary would act as an important 'memory jogger'. It would also serve as a reference source for anyone who wanted to know what date they had planted the peas last year or whatever. In fact, people got out of the habit of writing in the diary and the practice had totally ceased by the autumn of 1972.

Finances

However, whilst the members of Postlip relied on a few formalised arrangements for managing their every day activities, the management of their financial affairs was rather more formally laid down. Each family was responsible for its own domestic expense just like any other family in a conventional nuclear family set-up. However, as members of the Housing Association they did not formally own their homes. Rather the property was owned by the Association, to which legal entity they paid a 'rent'. As the living areas were of different sizes they did not pay equal shares of any communal bills such as electricity. The four units that together made up the actual hall each paid 21 per cent of communal costs, the occupants of the two cottages made up the rest by paying 8 per cent each. The bills of the community were handled by the treasurer of the Housing Association, who was Ian. The major expenditure of income was obviously the repayment of the mortgage obtained from the local council. As a condition of granting the mortgage, the local authority was allowed to nominate a representative to sit on the board of the Association. The members of the community had found this situation particularly irksome, especially at the time when they were involved in preparing the barn for their first concert and the local authority started getting very awkward about the lack of toilet facilities. Because of such interference and because they would be able to get a loan at a cheaper rate of interest, the Housing Association was going to apply for a mortgage from a building society in order to repay the local council and thereby ease them off their backs a little. The only other item of expenditure which they met together was the payment of the bills incurred by Chris's monthly trips to the wholesaler to purchase basic grocery items in bulk, whilst there was also a small car which was bought communally to enable the women to run the children to the local school and collect them in the afternoons. Naturally, for Postlip, John and Helen were not involved in this purchase as they had no children of school age and so, according to the Postlip way of looking at things, were not expected to contribute. The women took it in turns ferrying the children to school and back, such duties being performed primarily in their capacity as parents of children who were transported rather than in their capacity as female members of the community.

Problems and future prospects

From all this is might appear that Postlip Hall was little more than a glorified version of a micro-Span estate with a very active social life amongst the residents. In fact, the members did possess what is one of the defining characteristics of a community: they did think of themselves as a community, they did have a well-developed group consciousness which was strengthened by the apparent love they all shared for the house itself and its grounds. On top of this, the men particularly were involved together at weekends and in their spare time on the Society activities—the trout farming, the Tithe Barn and so on. Whether or not Postlip develops along the path leading to increased communality or whether they gradually retire completely into their separate and private homes and lives will depend very much on how they cope with the problems that they experience.

During the first months of their existence they were forced by the state of the building to live far more communally than they did by late 1972—cooking facilities were shared and a much greater amount of living space was communally used. This early period was the time when the group was concerned to gain publicity for its venture in order to attract new recruits. It was also the period which was dominated by the major problem of finance—the financial burden of converting the property into self-contained units, each with its own kitchen and other facilities, was far greater than they had anticipated. With the passing of this stage, with the needed number of people living there, with the reconstruction work largely completed, then the community passed into its second stage of life which had lasted up until the end of 1972. They had to an extent sought to withdraw from the public eye as they concentrated on launching the various ventures of the Society. They had also begun to appreciate the subtler aspects of communal living, including the problem of human relationships, with the passing of the first stage of excitement when little thought was paid to the possible hang-ups.

The advantages were real enough. As families they were living in a glorious part of England in a beautiful house which they had obtained for a price little more than they would have had to pay for a semi-detached home on a housing estate. In addition, they derived all the benefits that stem from having others around to share the chores of baby-sitting and the like. They also had company and friendship. The men had the physical space and the collective skills to pursue their Society ventures, whilst the women also seemed to find it a stimulating environment for their creative activities. Jane, for instance, had not painted for years before coming to Postlip although she trained at the Slade. Since living at Postlip she had started painting again, her work had been shown in a number of galleries and she had sold some of her paintings. Jay had found the creative energy to spend up to eight or ten hours a day working on her novels. The children also had fourteen acres of land to play in and kids of their own age with which to share it.

The advantages were, of course, only one side of the coin. The other side was not so rosy. Just as the children had companions with whom to play, so the parents had other sets of parents to disagree with about the children's behaviour. Thus, on the Sunday morning of my stay at Postlip I was woken by the screams and yells of kids running about the flat of Ian and Jane. I began to understand and temporarily sympathise with the complaint Chris had made to me the previous day that Jane was too lax with her children and didn't control them enough. Recovered after a nice breakfast and talking with Jane it transpired that she herself got upset by the way in which Jay, Chris's wife, would tell Jane's children off for doing things whereas the proper thing to do, she felt, would be to complain to Jane herself who would then see to the matter. The problem of commune members adhering to different principles and practices of child-rearing is fairly usual in communal groups where there are children, and one would expect that the conflict caused in this way would increase at Postlip as the children approached puberty.

Again, the men had the challenge and the pleasure of developing the new outside Society ventures, but this meant that they had correspondingly less time to spend with their wives who were left fulfilling the traditional female role of domestic. This experience of the wives contributed to the fear that some of them had that despite all the advantages of living at Postlip, and perhaps because of them, ordinary family life was suffering. Thus, they had friends and company at Postlip but this also meant that people were constantly calling round on other people, whether it was for a morning coffee or an evening's drink. The result was that couples sometimes felt that they no longer had sufficient time together as husband and wife. There was the feeling on the part of some of the members that the community had grown too close socially as a group at the cost of the traditional nuclear family group to which most of them were accustomed. It would appear that it was the women who felt this particularly, and in fact the females of the community would seem to have received a raw deal all the way round, for Chris and Jay's daughter complained that there were no girls of her age at the community.

The question of whether or not the group grows together more as a commune or drifts apart into a group of families living in close physical proximity to each other will obviously depend to an extent on how they cope with the problem of interpersonal differences and tensions of the sort referred to earlier. It will also depend on the resolution of another problem area that confronted Postlip as it has confronted other groups: the problem that stems from different members holding different definitions of the commune and different visions of its future. For at least some of the women at Postlip the future looked pretty much like the past, with each having her own private living area and only co-operating and sharing to a limited extent with the others. For at least one of the men, however, the future of Postlip was painted in terms of new ventures, each one eventually becoming financially self-supporting so that ultimately Postlip itself would be able to support those of the men who wished

Chapter 6

Centre of Light, Findhorn

A glance at the history of communal experiments of the past would reveal that the most successful groups in terms of longevity of life have had as their basis a shared religious belief or purpose. In Chapter 4 it was shown how the Kingsway Community in London was inspired in part at least by the religious commitment of its founder, David Horn. In the north of Scotland, on the Moray Firth, there is another inspired by a religious belief system—the Findhorn Community. Its origins can be traced to 1962 when Peter Caddy, his wife Eileen, their three sons, and a friend, Dorothy Maclean, moved into a caravan on a site at Findhorn in Morayshire in order to seek to create a new form of life for themselves. Peter, an ex-RAF officer had worked as the manager of a local hotel but then had been unable to find employment despite genuine efforts to do so. He began to work on a garden at the site and, in his words,[1]

> Then started the expansion, step by step, under God's guidance. We had to learn the laws of manifestation, for each one of us had given up all and were now entirely dependent upon God's limitless supply to meet our needs. As we became aware of a need, together we would ask that the need be met. We learnt that our united thought and our act of asking were both important to manifest our needs, and we gave thanks immediately knowing in complete faith that they would be manifested.

By 1969 this original nucleus had been joined by others and their number had grown to sixteen members. In that year they published a brief statement of their beliefs and the history of the group:[2]

H

The community at Findhorn consists of a group of people pioneering a new way of living. There are no blue prints; we seek and follow God's guidance which comes in different ways. The ability to receive God's guidance is available to all who take the time to be still and seek within. . . . My wife Eileen hears the still small voice within and receives detailed guidance which we have followed with astonishing results. In this way God has guided and directed all that is taking place in this community at Findhorn and in our lives. Of ourselves we are nothing but with God the seemingly impossible becomes possible.

We are living a way of life which is undenominational and therefore cannot be labelled. It is not an easy life, for ultimately it calls for total surrender of the self before that direct link with God can be firmly established. . . .

Our aim is to bring down the Kingdom of Heaven on earth and therefore everything must be as near perfect as possible, perfect to meet the need for which it is sought. To do this we have had to go ahead and do the seemingly impossible in implicit faith and trust, without any doubts, not restricted by what is in the bank but dependent on God's unlimited supply and His guidance for the needs of this ever expanding community. . . . We are pioneering a new way for the New Age which is gradually unfolding and will require a new type of man.

I first visited Findhorn during the early summer of 1969. I was met by Peter Caddy and it did not take him long to introduce me to the other members and the guests who were staying at the time. In all there were about 20 people living there in about four caravans, whilst the Caddys and a number of the older members occupied prefabricated bungalows constructed of cedar wood. In addition they had just completed the construction of their community centre which acted as dining hall, communal lounge and meeting area. The sanctuary had also been recently completed. When I returned in 1972 I was able to recognise a few of the older members and some of the original caravans and bungalows, but very little else. The community centre had been doubled in size. Land immediately adjacent to the original site had been 'colonised' by additional caravans and bungalows, whilst an additional site slightly to the north of the original had also been developed to provide space for living accommodation and for the workshops that had been developed since my first visit. The membership had grown to over a hundred full-time members.

The years 1969–72 had obviously brought about a tremendous growth and transformation of the venture. In this chapter I want to examine the ways in which Findhorn had changed.

The Findhorn belief system

In order to understand the ways in which Findhorn has developed it is necessary to understand the basic tenets of their belief system, for to a significant extent it is the flexibility of this set of beliefs that has enabled the leaders of the community to feel sufficiently free to reverse established policies and procedures, embark upon new projects, and direct the community along new pathways in response to and in anticipation of emergent problems confronting the venture.

Briefly, a number of key, first-order beliefs underpinning the Findhorn Centre of Light can be identified:

1   Man is involved in a process of cosmic evolutionary development which will lead to the establishment of a New Age, a new Heaven and a new Earth.
2   The source of this change is God, a Universal Presence, a Universal Energy Force, who is the Life within all things.
3   All people have a Divine Spirit to which they can attune if they take the time to be still and 'seek within'.
4   Because God is a Presence that is within all of us and whose voice can be heard by all, each can receive and obtain his own Divine inspiration or guidance and as a result there can be no such group as a 'spiritual élite' who possess a sacred hold over a single truth. Likewise, no distinction can be made between the 'saved' and the 'lost'. A more meaningful distinction is between those who have attuned to the Divine within themselves and are allowing the New Age energies to flow through them, living in the consciousness of the Oneness of life and working to serve the interests of the Whole, and those who are attuned to the old age, to the forces of materialism, seeing only their own interests and exploiting the Whole to satisfy their personal desires.
5   Because all men can attune to the Divine within them, because there is no spiritual élite, so also, each individual must choose his

own path. Each individual must act upon his own inner guidance, his own intuitive powers. Thus, whilst the individual is required to translate his vision into the realm of daily existence in order to encourage others to attune to the Divine within themselves, no blueprint for the forms and structures of the New Age is recognised.
6   At the same time, the individual and collective task of those attuned to the New Age is to create a new culture, but as the major creative force in the world is man's consciousness, this project is to be achieved not by attacking Old Age forms of life but by creating positive alternatives to the old which can act to inspire others with the vision of a New Age.
7   This is the major function of Findhorn which, as a Centre of Light, has the aim of bringing down the Kingdom of Heaven onto Earth.

Thus, the prime injunction for those who wish to work towards the creation of a New Age is to attune to the Divine within themselves and in faith act upon the guidance received in a spirit of Love but which is at the same time balanced by Truth, 'the exercise of that faculty of discrimination that sees what is the right action at any given time . . . and prevents the energy of Love from being dissipated over too wide a field or from being taken advantage of'.[3]

As part of its aim of bringing down the Kingdom of Heaven to Earth, of being instrumental in the creation of a New Age, Findhorn is seen as having a number of more specific functions. Prime amongst these is the demonstration to the rest of the world of how to work harmoniously with the inhabitants of what the people at Findhorn refer to as the 'elemental world': the Devas and the Nature Spirits. The results that are obtained in the gardens of Findhorn in terms of the quality of the flowers and vegetables are explained in terms of the co-operation that is practised between the beings of three planes of existence: Man, the Devas, and the Nature Spirits.

'Man', the organiser and practical creator of the garden is represented by Peter Caddy and the members of the community with special responsibility for tending to the gardens. 'The Devas are the Angelic Beings who wield the archetypal forces. There is one of these for every species of the plant kingdom and in addition there are Devas of sound, colour, wind, etc.' Dorothy Maclean, whose spiritual name in Divina, is the main communicator with these architects of the 'elemental world'. 'Consultations' are held with these beings, and their advice is sought concerning the garden. Whereas the Devas are considered as providing the blueprint for the plant world, the Nature Spirits are seen as carrying out the actual work. These Nature Spirits, under the leadership of Pan, the God of Nature, communicate with the people at Findhorn through a 'sensitive' known at the community as Roc. It is to Roc that Pan has manifested himself on many occasions and in many places. The function of Findhorn, according to Pan, is to show to Man that he must work in co-operation with the Nature Spirits and the Devas if the earth is not to be turned into a polluted and ruined desert as a result of ecological disaster. Thus,[4]

> The world of nature spirits is sick of the way man is treating the life forces. They [the Devas and elementals] are working with God's law in plant growth. Man is continually violating it. There is a real likelihood that they may even turn their back on man whom they sometimes consider to be a parasite on earth. This could mean a withdrawal of life force from the plant forms, with obviously devastating results.
>
> Yet their wish is to work in co-operation with man who has been given a divine task of tending the earth. For generations man has ignored them and even denied their existence. Now a group of men consciously invite them to their garden. . . . The delight in the Deva world is apparently great. At last men have begun to wake up. Since the spiritual world is all one, a great living unity, the news shoots around instantly and the devas throng in with joy to help.
>
> They are literally demonstrating that the desert can blossom as the rose. They also show the astonishing pace at which this can be brought about. If this can be done so quickly at Findhorn, it can be done in the Sahara. If enough men could really begin to use this co-operation consciously, food could be grown in quantity on the most infertile areas. There is virtually no limit if 'factor x' can be brought into play on top of our organic methods. . . .

Throughout the life of the community a major role has been played by Eileen Caddy, whose spiritual name is Elixer. Since 1962 she has received guidance from God concerning the life and the developments at Findhorn. In 1969 she received guidance concerning the future growth and expansion:[5]

My beloved, I want you to see this Centre of Light as an ever growing cell of Light. It has started as a family group, is now a community, will grow into a village, then into a town and finally into a vast City of Light. It will progress in stages and expand very rapidly. Expand with the expansion. . . . Let go of all fear of it becoming out of hand. I can assure you it will not, but will grow and flourish and flower and glorious will be the results for all to see and all will recognise My Hand in everything that is taking place. Let everything unfold quite naturally. . . .

It is time to look at how Findhorn has flourished and flowered since then.

Membership and recruitment

In 1969–70 when the membership of the group was only a couple of dozen they had no formal recruitment policy. Typically, people would come on a visit and if sufficiently impressed would seek to stay on to become a permanent member. They were expected to supply their own accommodation and pay the rates and ground rent and other costs incurred through their occupying a caravan or bungalow. Those young members who could not afford such an initial outlay but who had skills to offer were housed in a seven-berth caravan that had been bought for the community for that purpose and received small amounts of pocket money on an *ad hoc* basis. At the same time as pursuing a fairly 'open-door' kind of recruitment policy, this was tempered, as are all things at Findhorn, by a practical element—that is, it was made clear to potential members that the community had neither the energy, the time, nor the desire to accept as members those who were incapable of making a contribution to the life of the community. Thus, Peter Caddy wrote in 1970:[6]

> I can only emphasise strongly that this is a working group and all must contribute both financially and of their skills and gifts. We need dedicated people capable of making a useful contribution, whether it be in the office, the garden, cooking, plumbing, electrical work etc.

By the summer of 1971 the membership had grown to forty-five adults and ten children. By the following summer the total membership number had passed the 100 mark. These new members have been drawn from a variety of walks of life. Many have come from the ranks of the spiritual/mystical wing of the international youth culture who heard about Findhorn from friends, through reading the literature published by Findhorn or possibly through attending one of the conferences on spiritual matters in which representatives of Findhorn have participated or organised. Other members would appear to have been drawn from the ranks of the relatively affluent middle class who have usually found their way to Findhorn through a long-term involvement in religious and esoteric groups such as the Theosophists, or else through following friends or relatives who have travelled this path and have been led to live at Findhorn. In 1973 Findhorn also received its first local recruit, a retired bank manager living in the neighbourhood who, over time, got to know the members of the community and eventually decided to join.

This expansion in the numbers living at Findhorn has been partly the cause and partly the result of the expansion in the range of activities pursued by the members of the community. Up until 1970 the activities of the members were devoted largely to tending the two acres of garden, producing literature, and carrying out correspondence and dealing with visitors. In addition a workshop had been established and frequently a proportion of the membership would be involved in construction work such as preparing sites for the caravans and bungalows of new members. However, among the new members who were drawn to Findhorn were many young artists and craftsmen, although there were no arts or craft activities organised by the community as such at that time. But in 1969 Eileen had received a vision of the arts and crafts centre to be developed by the community. By October 1971 this centre had been constructed. The activities in pottery, weaving, and other crafts were now run as a business enterprise, Findhorn Studios Ltd. The items produced were sold in the craft shop run by the community and in shops throughout Britain.

In the arts the period 1969–72 saw the growth of a folk singing group that performed outside the community and in the small theatre that was constructed by the community members through converting a small shop on the camp-site. The dramatic group and the various musical and dance groups also performed there. In addition to the development of the arts and crafts, the publishing activities at Findhorn were greatly expanded, to the extent that a new print shop was to be built at an estimated cost of £30,000 fully equipped. An educational venture had also been started with the purchase of a house that was owned by the proprietor of the caravan site where a college was in the process of being established.

The formation of this college provides an excellent example of the way in which new developments took place at Findhorn in response to a variety of problems and opportunities that have emerged. The influx of artists to the community had led to the formation of *ad hoc* artist workshops, but these were limited by a lack of adequate space and accommodation. People started thinking about the desirability of having proper classrooms. Then, in the summer of 1970 David Spangler and his associate Myrtle Glines arrived at the community from America. David was immediately recognised as a spiritual authority and began a series of lectures on the New Age. This was the first time any kind of educational activity had taken place at Findhorn. Myrtle had training as a teacher and counsellor in human relations and began to hold classes which developed into discussion groups for the purpose of examining the experiences and challenges that community living created. At the same time many young people were arriving at Findhorn who, it was felt, lacked a deep grounding in the spiritual insights upon which the community was founded, and it was believed that these people would benefit from instruction. Young people also arrived at Findhorn from schools where esoteric and spiritual principles were taught, and this made the people at Findhorn realise more fully the importance of the community as a training centre for young people.

The money to buy the property suitable to house the anticipated college was 'manifested' through a new member of the community who donated the sum of £12,000 which she had been left in her husband's will. At the same time the establishment of the college was influenced by the more practical issues of finance: once the college was begun it was hoped that Findhorn would be able to gain, in the eyes of the Inland Revenue, the charitable status as an educational institute which it had been seeking for a number of years. Moreover, once a college had been established it was felt that the function of Findhorn as a training centre for the young would be facilitated as American students would then be able to obtain travel grants and scholarships to come to Findhorn.

By 1972, with the successful attainment of charitable status, the relatively open recruitment policy that had characterised Findhorn up to that time underwent a change as a consequence of the growth in the size of the membership and as a response to the many letters that were, and are, received daily from people seeking to join the venture. A ruling was made that[7]

> When people come to stay, they must go through a probationary period of not less than three months during which time they have the opportunity to integrate with the whole. If they do this successfully, then they must provide their own accommodation and continue to cover their living expenses. These are the basic requirements for new members, although as always the guidance is that we are to be flexible.

Flexibility was indeed the actual practice, for approximately half the membership were young people with limited means to whom the community made some contribution towards their living expenses. In practice, whether a person was allowed to stay on as a member or not depended entirely on Peter Caddy's decision. This development on the one hand of more formalised procedures and articulated policies to deal with problems and situations, and on the other hand the actual implementation of such policies depending upon the decision of Peter Caddy, which meant that no consistent standardised practice ever emerged, was a thread common to all areas of life at Findhorn.

Relations with the outside world

The people at Findhorn could be considered as a cognitive minority adhering to a view of the world and a life style significantly different from the cognitive majority that surround them. As such, their relationships with such outsiders had a significant effect on their own way of life and exerted a determining influence on their development. As one would perhaps expect from a group whose belief system is such as to allow great flexibility with regard to what might be termed the 'second order' principles directing their daily existence, the development of Findhorn over the last ten years in terms of its relationships with the wider society and its members has not followed a single, consistent path. One of the consequences of leading a life directed by God is that His guidance and hence one's policies and actions based on such communications can change over time. In considering this aspect of Findhorn's existence I shall concentrate on two areas—first, the changes in their relationships with 'non-believers' in the wider society, and second, the related changes in their policies towards the 'interested sympathisers' made up of visitors to the community and those receiving their literature.

1   Relations with 'non-believers'

When I first visited the community in 1969 I think it would be true to say that they were much concerned to shield the nature of their activities from the local inhabitants of the area. They made no attempt to convert them to their belief system and way of life. Not only did they feel that any attempt to proselytise would be wasted, they also believed that all who were led to seek the light would eventually be attracted towards Findhorn.

Up until 1969 the proselytising activities of Findhorn had been confined mainly to publishing literature and receiving those visitors who had heard of the venture in esoteric circles or through the 'underground circuit'. However, in that year they had agreed to take part in a television programme on the 'alternative society' on the basis of guidance received by Eileen, that 'Only the very best can come out of the publicity through the BBC. . . . Great things are coming to pass. . . . This is a time of great joy and uplift, a moving ahead into a completely new phase of the work. . . .'[8] In 1970 further indication of a change in policy with regard to relationships with the outside world was contained in a letter I received from Peter Caddy in which he wrote, 'We can no longer hide our light under a bushel and, now that we are firmly established, the time has come for information about us to be spread far and wide.'

Thus, by 1972 a complete transformation had taken place in the orientation of Findhorn towards those of the outside world who did not share their belief system. In retrospect, and on the basis of guidance received, they claimed that their relative isolation during the early years was important in providing them with the opportunity to build the foundations of the centre. Moreover, it was felt that during the early years of existence their links with the Nature Spirits and such like were not the kinds of experiences that could easily be shared with those committed to a more mundane view of the world. Apart from guidance received, three developments were seen as significant by the people of Findhorn in bringing about the change in their orientation:

a In 1971 a few of the members of the community were teaching in local schools as a means of earning their livelihood. A number of local parents expressed concern about this as rumours were spreading about 'sex and drug orgies' at the community. To counter this Peter Caddy invited reporters from two regional newspapers to visit the community. The result was the appearance in the papers of glowing reports about the orderliness, the cleanliness and the beauty of the community and the apparent normality of the people living there. As a consequence, local people began to visit the community, although by 1973 only one had actually joined.[9]

b A few weeks after the appearance of the newspaper articles Findhorn was featured in a half-hour programme on Scottish BBC. Again, the picture portrayed of Findhorn was very favourable and, as Peter Caddy has written, 'It laid to rest forever the image of our being a hippie commune and demonstrated for all who watched that we were a place of happy people truly building toward an alternative society.'[10]

c Not long after the television programme, the public opening of the Findhorn Studios was held. At the ceremony to bless the new venture local clergymen and other 'dignitaries' were invited to attend and participate. This provided another indication of the concern of the people at Findhorn to break down the barriers between themselves and the local populace. Moreover, with the development of the craft studios and the dramatic and artistic activities at the community it was felt that the possibility of meaningful communication with the outside world was made more realistic. Thus,[11]

> The message of the New Age, of joy and of greater attunement
> to the whole of Life, which might not be accepted in terms of
> working with Nature Spirits or being a Light Centre, could
> find new outlets, new forms of communication through the
> universal language of art. . . . This was the dream behind the
> vision and building of Findhorn Studios: that this new
> enterprise would be a powerful link between the inner aspects of
> Findhorn life and work and the outside school.

Hence, the sale of goods to the public, particularly through the shop they ran on the caravan site, was not seen solely in terms of producing an income for the community but was also considered as an important communication link for spreading the word and the example of Findhorn. The performances of the theatre group, the choirs and musical groups were viewed in a similar manner. When they performed for people from outside the community, such as at local schools and at the RAF base sited next to the community, their aim was not solely to entertain, but also to spread the message.[12] One of the consequences of Findhorn 'going public' in this way was that as knowledge of their existence spread in this country and abroad, so the flow of visitors and potential recruits to the centre increased. This factor can be seen as significant in understanding the changes that have taken place with regard to the policies concerning visitors and the readers of their literature.

2   *Visitors and the mailing list*

In 1969 the community received approximately 600 visitors. The policy was that no one was to be invited to come to Findhorn and no one was to be turned away when they arrived. Furthermore, as God would provide, the visitors were not charged any specific sum. Rather it was left up to them to donate whatever they wished as repayment for the hospitality they had received. In addition, literature was sent out completely free of charge to all those who requested it. However, during 1971 the number of annual visitors had risen to 1,500 and there were over 3,000 on the mailing list.

Undoubtedly this increased flow of visitors can be attributed, just as can the increase in membership, to the publicity obtained by Findhorn over this period. Moreover, the large number of visitors, many of them young people with limited financial resources, and the large number in receipt of the literature, must have represented a considerable financial burden upon Findhorn. Thus, given the flexibility allowed by the general principles of the belief system with its major injunction to listen to the voice of God within, one might reasonably have expected a change in policy to occur. By 1972, in fact, these policies had been completely reversed. Visitors were now charged a fixed rate during their stay. They were required to book in advance and people who turned up unannounced were frequently turned away. In addition, Findhorn began to charge for many of its publications and on attaining charitable status began to charge those who wished to be placed on their mailing list. The occasion for this apparent tightening-up of policy can once again be traced to the direct spiritual guidance received by Elixer and David Spangler.[13]

Since the guidance received involved a radical departure from that previously obtained, it is worth looking in some detail at the processes which led up to the change. As the publicity received by Findhorn increased, so did the numbers of those who wished to receive the literature. This involved not only a financial burden but also required the expenditure of a great deal of energy. Discussions began to take place about the wasted costs and energy involved in sending out material to people who never replied or sent donations in return. David Spangler sought guidance on this issue. In 1970 he wrote a short but significant pamphlet, *New Age Energies and New Age Laws*, in which he argued that we were entering a new age of consciousness and activity in which new energy forces were becoming operative. Such New Age energies required New Age laws to control their use. Four laws were listed, and of these the third proved to have a significant consequence for the nature of Findhorn's relationships with the outside world as represented by the people on their mailing list. As this law was expressed:[14]

> All energies that flow out from a centre must return to that
> centre to complete the cycle. Also, energies received by a centre
> must be balanced by a commensurate outflow from that
> centre.

As the publishing and mailing of literature was one of the main vehicles at Findhorn for spreading New Age energies, the implementation of this law required a change in policy. Money was considered to be one form of energy. That flow of energy from Findhorn in the form of literature should return in the form of money.[15] By June 1972 the policy of a yearly subscription to the Findhorn mailing list was established.

It was in 1972, on the occasion of Findhorn attaining charitable status, that a change of policy with regard to visitors was implemented. Again, the basic flexibility of a belief system where the prime injunction is to act upon the guidance received from the Divine within was revealed. Thus, on 4 March 1972 Eileen Caddy received the following guidance:[16]

> Because in the past it has been right to make no charge and
> simply to allow each one to contribute whatever he could give, it
> does not mean now, with the expansion and increased
> responsibilities of the community, that it is right for this
> policy to remain static. Like so many things, this can be and has

been abused by some; therefore the time has come when changes are necessary and this is the time for these changes to take place. . . . It will be necessary at this time to be very flexible, but the general policy should be a minimum charge of £2 per day per person. Remember, because this is right, only the right people will come. This is not a hippie commune and nothing should be taken for granted. You will find that with this change of policy, this Centre of Light will be appreciated far, far more by the many. So go ahead in complete confidence and ignore all opposition.

In a pamphlet, *Findhorn and Finance*, this change of policy was discussed at some length, and apart from stating that the prime reason for the change in policy was that it was guided by God, other reasons were mentioned. The decision was justified in terms of the New Age law of energy circulation referred to above. Reference was also made to the great financial burden presented by the numbers of young people living at Findhorn with no source of regular income who had to be supported by the community. Reference to the expanded activities of Findhorn in the fields of the arts was made. This was another financial responsibility. Another problem faced by Findhorn which the new policy was intended to meet was that concerning the increasing numbers of people who sought to visit Findhorn and the decreasing amount of space that was available to accommodate them as the permanent membership grew in size. So, 'let those who wish to come be the means by which God can manifest accommodation. Let visitors and potential visitors contribute to a fund for increased accommodation.'[17] The charging of visitors was also justified in terms of establishing a barrier to the increasing numbers of merely curious sightseers who had started arriving following publicity received by Findhorn on Scottish Television and in the regional newspapers. Finally, those who could not afford to pay the charges were asked to put their faith into practice and have trust that God would manifest the answers to their needs. In this way the new policy was seen as furthering the ultimate goal of Findhorn, for through the personal experience of God thus obtained, such people 'will become living citizens of a New Age and hasten by that much the day when all mankind will know again the Oneness of God'.[18]

So, it is possible to discern with regard to the change in policy concerning the charging of visitors a response to a number of problems stemming from the increased size and range of activities of the community, which led to an increased financial burden and to a lack of sufficient accommodation for the increased numbers of visitors. At the same time, Divine guidance was received for this policy, and it was also justified in terms of promoting the ultimate goal of the Centre. For the people at Findhorn, the prime reason for change in policy was the guidance received from God; for the sociologist it might appear that such guidance merely provided the legitimation necessary to justify a change in policy forced upon the community by problems of numbers, extended activities, finance and limited space. One's position on such a question must surely depend upon the nature of the world one sees oneself as occupying, and the purpose of this chapter is not one of questioning the world of those at Findhorn.

Organisation

Unlike many communities of the past which have been destroyed by conflicts over authority between the members, Findhorn has been spared such experiences to a very large extent due to the ability of Eileen Caddy to 'hear the still small voice within' and receive detailed guidance on any question upon which direction was sought. If Eileen has been the one who heard the voice of God, it has been Peter Caddy's task to implement the will of God in practice. Particularly in the period up to 1970 the driving force behind the community was Peter Caddy, aided by Eileen who obtained the necessary guidance from God and by other 'sensitives' such as the member who could communicate with the Nature Spirits and the Edinburgh friend of the community who was able to warn Findhorn whenever it was threatened by dark forces. Peter was the man who made all the decisions, ranging from who should be allowed to stay and who not to, what new ventures and construction schemes should be embarked upon and who should perform what task. He escorted the visitors around the community, gave introductory talks, worked in the garden, and dealt with the correspondence and general administrative tasks that were required. In other words, the organisational style was that typically associated with the rule of a charismatic leader.

The growth in the size of the community, the expansion of its

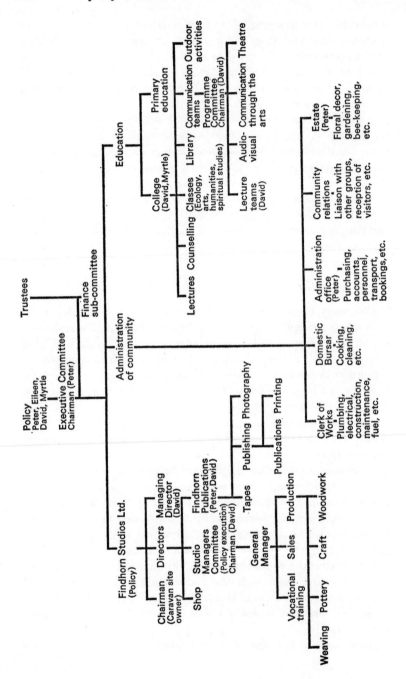

range of activities and its changed legal status would lead, one would expect, to a certain routinisation of the authority relationships and decision-making procedures within the community. At the formal level this appeared to have been what happened. On paper at least Findhorn came to be characterised by a hierarchically organised structure of authority, with each area of activity having a single person in charge and with Peter acting as over-all co-ordinator and inspirer of new ventures (see organisational chart opposite).

The overall policy of spiritual direction was decided by Peter and Eileen in consultation with David Spangler and Myrtle Glines. The heads of departments were increasingly taking charge of the day-to-day running of the community. The Executive Committee met once a month to decide on matters of policy concerning the community. These decisions then were announced to the gathering of the community as a whole which also took place once a month. The purpose of this latter meeting was simply one of communication —no votes were taken on the policies announced. The role of the trustees was seen basically as one of clearing up the legal and financial 'loose ends' left in the wake of Peter acting under 'guidance', unrestrained by conventional business considerations.

All Heads of Departments, such as the Clerk of Works and Domestic Bursar were 'appointed' by Peter. As with all his decisions, the choice was made on the basis of his own intuitive judgment, occasionally with the aid of guidance received by either Eileen or David Spangler. Thus, it can be seen that although a more routinised pattern of administration appeared to be emerging at Findhorn, the charisma possessed by the spiritual leaders of the community influenced the operation of the community at all levels. Moreover, at the same time as the structures for dealing in a regularised fashion with the routine problems of daily existence in the community developed, with an increase in the division of labour, specialisation of tasks, and a 'top-down' authority flow, a counter-trend has also developed at Findhorn over the recent period.

Fundamental to the Findhorn belief system is the assertion that everyone can receive his own guidance if he takes the trouble to be still and listen to the voice of the Divine within, whether this is heard in the form of intuition or as an actual voice. Although this has always been an article of faith along with the rejection of any idea of a spiritual élite, in the early years of the community this was rarely practised at the level of the practical organisation of the

I

community. As with other community groups of the past with a strong mystical element in their belief system, control and authority was exercised solely by those whose consciousnesses were the most highly developed in terms of their ability to attune to the voice of God. In the case of Findhorn up until 1970 this authority was exercised solely by Peter Caddy with the support of Eileen. Since 1970, however, there would appear to have been a gradual change in this area. As one of the community members has written:[19]

> It is by no means a one-man, or a one-couple band, even if hitherto it has been run pretty much on authoritarian lines. The expansion has brought in a number of people of very independent spirit, and their role is acknowledged in a programme of devolution and decentralisation that is now under way. . . .
> A key figure in the programme has been a young American teacher named David Spangler, who arrived in the summer of 1970, and was at once accepted as a spiritual authority. He has helped to steer the community into a recognition that everyone has access to 'guidance', though not necessarily in the same dramatic form as Eileen and that everyone must learn to hold responsibility, though not necessarily in the same forceful style as Peter. In other words, the development is towards an acceptance of the need for spiritual self-reliance (though self is not the word), and in a context, increasingly, of social self-reliance.

In understanding the processes involved in this development it is obviously necessary to take account of the influx of new people, many with special skills and abilities, who were able to exercise authority in their own area of expertise (for instance, at the time of writing, the Clerk of Works was a foreman on a building site before coming to Findhorn). Furthermore, the rapid expansion in the size of Findhorn and in the range of activities pursued there meant that Peter was no longer able to exercise a strict supervision over every aspect of life at the community. He was 'forced' to delegate authority to other members. In addition, the influence that David Spangler had over the community as a whole and over Peter in particular in leading to a certain amount of decentralisation was also important. However, as with so many things at Findhorn, the final seal was laid on this development by God speaking through Eileen. Thus, one of the most significant events occurred in October 1971. Prior to this Eileen had received guidance for the community which was read out each morning in the sanctuary. This practice ceased as a regular event following a message received by Eileen on 20 October 1971 which confirmed that henceforth the emphasis should be on the members of the community as a whole developing their ability to receive guidance to direct their activities:[20]

> My beloved, now is the perfect time for a complete change of rhythm for you. It is no longer necessary for you to receive a message from Me each day for the community and for the manu. For a very long time I have gone on day after day repeating Myself; it is now time My word was lived and demonstrated. . . . You cannot spoonfeed a child all its life. The time comes when it has to learn to feed itself and you have to let it do so. Let go and stand back and allow all those in the community to live a life guided and directed by Me.

In addition, the Caddys also received guidance that by 1974 the community should have developed to a stage where it would be possible for Peter and Eileen to leave the group for periods of time while they travelled around other Centres of Light throughout the world. They therefore became very concerned to encourage individuals to develop their 'sense of responsibility' and their ability to organise and make decisions.

However, whilst there was a conscious change in the nature of authority relationships at Findhorn and whilst many members spoke to me of the increased 'freedom' they were appreciating, all the major decisions and many of the minor ones were either made by Peter or by Heads of Departments after consultation with Peter. Whenever Peter himself felt the need for spiritual guidance from other sources he obtained a 'reading' from either Eileen or David Spangler.

The daily routine at Findhorn

It was constantly stressed to the visitor at Findhorn that it was a 'working community'. This fact was certainly reflected in their daily routine. The members' day commenced with breakfast in their own caravans or bungalows. Sanctuary was at eight-thirty. This consisted of a short period of silent meditation, usually followed by Eileen and other members of the community sharing with the others their guidance or visions that they had received. This was then followed by the announcements concerning the events of the day by Peter and the Heads of Departments. After the first morning session in the sanctuary (due to the increase in the number of visitors a second session had been started which took place at nine-fifteen) Peter was usually to be found positioned at a convenient point for others to have a word with him about some issue or other. Work commenced around nine-thirty and continued until twelve-thirty when there was the vegetarian lunch. Work recommenced about two and continued until approximately four-fifteen when people broke off to have afternoon tea either in their own dwelling or with others. Between five and seven when the evening meal took place people either continued working or else were involved in rehearsals or some kind of educational activity. In the evening there was sanctuary which was usually followed by some form of community activity such as a lecture, discussion groups, a 'fun night', etc.

This pattern of daily activities, which was printed out on a notice in the community centre, was adhered to on every day, although one member informed me that there was a certain 'slacking off' on Sundays which he interpreted as the first hint that the institution of the 'weekend' was beginning to emerge. However, to the visitor or new member who expressed surprise at the hours of work expected of people at Findhorn it was explained that work is 'love in action' and the willingness to work was considered as a practical demonstration of one's commitment to Findhorn and its ideals. Anyone who was reluctant to work, like the retired couple who declared that as they were retired they were only prepared to work during the mornings, was considered to be not yet ready for the responsibilities of community living and Findhorn was not the place for them.

The day of the new member or visitor was fairly similar to that followed by the established members except that they were expected to participate in a fairly intensive socialisation process involving guided tours around the community, tape-recorded lectures every day, question and answer sessions with community members, slide shows with recorded commentaries, and such like.

Basically, this daily pattern did not appear to have changed much since early 1970 except for the increased amount of time spent on cultural and educational activities, something which was completely absent on my first visit. However, the system had become more formalised and as the division of labour had increased with the accompanying specialisation a significant change had taken place.

On my first visit one of the members told me how one of the things he liked about life at Findhorn was that he did a different thing every day. This was not something many people could claim by the time of my second visit.

Finance

Just as the passage of time and the accompanying growth in the size and range of activities at Findhorn had led to attempts to routinise to some extent the patterns of organisation and work, so attempts had also been made to regularise the financial side of life.

Prior to 1970 the only form of financial support received by the community was donations from outsiders and from the wealthier members of the community. Concern was never revealed about any lack of money in the bank whenever a new venture was embarked upon. Implicit faith in the laws of manifestation coupled with the belief that 'only the best was good enough for God' meant that expenditure was never curtailed for financial considerations. In fact, the money necessary to meet the bills incurred by new buildings and new equipment always arrived from some source or another and so the faith of the members in the laws of manifestation was reinforced again and again. This pattern provides an ideal illustration of Weber's characterisation of the charismatic leader as one who despises 'traditional or rational everyday economising, the attainment of a regular income by continuous economic activity devoted to this end'.[21]

With the rapid growth in numbers and expansion of the building programme to house the new ventures, the faith in God's supply through donations was supplemented by a concern to provide a more regular and predictable source of income. So much so that one of the leading members of the community expressed to me his belief that the establishment of a stable financial basis for the community was one of the most important themes in its new phase of growth. Developments at Findhorn in the financial sphere appeared to bear out Weber's assertion that: 'For charisma to be transformed into a permanent routine structure, it is necessary that it's anti-economic character should be altered. It must be adapted to some forms of fiscal organisation to provide for the needs of the group. . . .'[22]

Thus, reference has already been made to the financial considerations that lay behind the introduction of set charges for the literature and for visitors. Income was also obtained through the craft studios and craft shop, the supermarket that the community ran on the caravan site, and the theatre. Financial considerations were also very much to the fore with regard to the attainment of charitable status. This meant that the trust was not liable for Income Tax on its earnings, received rating concessions on its buildings, was eligible to claim the Income Tax paid by covenanters on fixed sums deeded to the trust, and was exempted from Estate Duty on all gifts up to the sum of £50,000. The fact that they had been promised an estate in the Lake District on the death of its owner meant that they would certainly obtain very practical financial advantages from their new-found legal status.

As has been remarked, one of the key themes at Findhorn at this stage of development, in the light of the community's function as a training centre for New Age people, was the emphasis on individuals developing their own ability to receive guidance, to employ the New Age energies involved in the laws of manifestation, and to develop their own 'social self-reliance'. It was within the context of this orientation that the plan to make each department of the community financially self-supporting was explained and justified. The aim at the time of my second visit was that the craft studios, the printing venture, the photographic section, the theatre group, the gardens and so on should eventually be responsible for supplying their own financial needs. Thus, it was anticipated that the gardeners would be responsible for establishing a solid financial base for their activities through the sale of plants, shrubs, etc. to the public and to the other members of the community. This change in emphasis whereby activities which were originally started to provide supportive services for the community as such were now considered more as business ventures within the context of the community as a whole was evidenced by the financial report drawn up for the photographic side of the 'Findhorn Studios Ltd' where it was clearly stated that 'during the first eighteen months the department changed from an internal service organisation to where it is now, the object to make it a financially viable unit'. Despite this, the continued dependence of the various departments upon the manifestation of money through donors was revealed in the same report: in the first nine months of operation 90 per cent of the capital expansion was financed through donations which had totalled nearly £1,750 after eighteen months.

Future prospects

In examining the changes in the organisation and running of Findhorn as a Centre of Light, emphasis has been placed upon the constraints imposed by a rapid growth in numbers upon the life of what was originally a small group of believers living together as a community. Amongst other things this growth in numbers made possible an expansion in the range of activities pursued by the community, which in turn increased the 'space' available for new recruits. In responding to the pressures stemming from such developments, the 'significant others' at Findhorn brought about a number of changes in the way life was ordered both within the community and with regard to the community's relations with the wider society surrounding it. This transformation had, however, been made relatively 'easily' due to the essential flexibility of the belief system of Findhorn with its prime injunction to listen to the voice of the Divine that can be attuned to by all who seek to develop the ability (coupled with the ability of key members such as Eileen Caddy to obtain Divine support, guidance and legitimation, for the changes that had taken place). As a consequence, whilst the general trend revealed over the last few years at Findhorn was one of routinisation with an increased emphasis on the division of labour, the development of a formal authority structure, the concern to build up a stable financial basis and so on, the emergence of a completely bureaucratised style of organisation was countered by the emphasis upon the charismatic powers of all the members in general, and the powers of such people as the Caddys in particular.

However, the recognition of the charisma of all members would seem to involve an inevitable degree of conflict with the apparently felt need to develop permanent routine structure for dealing with the everyday needs and conditions involved in living as a community of 'cognitive deviants'. It is to such tensions that exist within the present system and the possible responses to them that one of the keys to future developments at Findhorn must be sought. Before turning attention to a consideration of the existing and potential sources of conflict and tension at Findhorn, it should be made clear that the members themselves had little doubt about the future of the community: expansion so that the existing community became a 'City of Light', and continued revelation of the active 'Presence of the Beloved' within all which links 'us together in the Oneness of all upon the Earth and in the opportunity to serve that Oneness until it becomes demonstrated in all lives throughout the world'.[23]

1   *Intuition v. routine*

Whenever Peter Caddy received guidance that new equipment or the creation of a new venture was called for, then he felt the need to go ahead with this, unrestrained by conventional considerations about available finance or manpower and other 'practical considerations'. This meant that he frequently ignored the routines and conventions of organisational administration, with the result that conflict was not infrequent with the trustees who had the ultimate responsibility in the eyes of the world if anything went wrong and who were accustomed to the Old Age ways of going about things. This conflict was kept within bounds at the time of writing because final recourse could be made to Eileen who could obtain guidance from the ultimate source—you just do not argue with God. However, if the business ventures of Findhorn continue to expand then the pressures from the business-oriented trustees on those who place all their faith in God and His abundant supply of needed resources could increase. So long as the Caddys remain at Findhorn the victory of routine business methods and considerations over the methods of inspiration, 'hunch' and 'guidance' will be denied. Developments after this would depend on the personal strengths and qualities of the future 'custodians' of the community.

2   *New Age culture v. Old Age business*

Just as there was a certain amount of conflict at Findhorn arising from the inspirational methods adhered to by Peter and the methods favoured by the trustees which take account of 'practical' considerations, there was also a certain amount of tension between the twin aims governing the running of the various departments such as the studios. This was revealed in the guidance received by David Spangler:[24]

> The purpose of the Findhorn Studios as a business is to assist in the circulation to and from this centre of the energy known as money, but that is not its primary function. It is primarily another means through which a greater consciousness of service, of love, of beauty and of revelation can manifest itself into the

human condition. . . . You must know that you are not
creating an economic device designed to place you into a
competitive state. You are creating an artistic device designed
to reveal, to make manifest, to illumine, to uplift and to
inspire. . . . Your objective as a business is not exactly the same
as the objective of a business in the outer world, which is to
enhance its economic and competitive position. Your objective
is to release to the world that which will bless and transform it.

The problem here was one of striking the right balance between these
two aims. Conflict had arisen in the past over the decision that
members of the community must purchase goods from the studio at
retail prices. The possibility was that such financial considerations
would grow to outweigh the concern with spreading the example of
a New Age, with the likelihood that Findhorn would follow the path
taken by the Oneida community in the United States which ended
up as just another profitable business enterprise, although a verbal
commitment to the New Age culture might remain. Certainly, dis-
quiet had been expressed by certain members at the way in which
financial considerations influenced the introduction of charges for
visitors, the establishment of the college in order to attain charitable
status for the community, and so on. However, the business enterprises at Findhorn did differ from conventional business organisations in one significant way—they were run on the basis of 'from each
according to his ability, to each according to his need', although as
has been pointed out members did not practise the common ownership of all worldly goods.

3   Centralisation v. dispersion of spiritual authority

Whilst the ability of Eileen to communicate with God and thereby
obtain the 'final word' on all matters of dispute within the community meant that Findhorn could avoid many of the conflicts
which have plagued other communities, the emphasis on the ability
of all to receive guidance from God and the rejection of any spiritual
élite could be seen as conflicting somewhat with the actual practice
at Findhorn where Eileen and Peter made the final decision on so
many things and where David Spangler in particular was considered
by many of the members as possessing the status of a 'guru'. The
possibility of people obtaining conflicting guidance was obviously a
potential source of stress and tension within the community. This

problem was resolved at Findhorn in a number of ways. First of all, a 'spiritual hierarchy' was recognised. If one of the members of the community kept announcing that he had received guidance that he was to pursue some course of action, and if, for instance, that course of action appeared to involve the expansion of his own personal area of control and influence within the community, then guidance would be sought by Eileen on the matter from her own source. If her guidance conflicted with that claimed by the individual, credence was given to Eileen's information and it was assumed that the other individual was operating from the selfish, egoistic, 'personality level', projecting his own desires and wants in his imagined guidance which in fact stemmed from his *sub*-conscious rather than his higher consciousness. If such a person persisted in claiming to receive guidance that conflicted with that received by the 'spiritual leaders', then it would be decided by Peter that Findhorn was not the right place for the person and he would have to leave. The police had been called to assist in the past when one member refused to leave when asked to do so.

Obviously, the possibility of a split developing within the community would be much greater if conflicting guidance was received by any of what could be termed the 'spiritual leaders' of the community. As far as I could discover this had occurred only once in the past. Partly this was because there was a kind of division of labour between the 'sensitives'. Peter would seek a 'reading' from different 'sensitives' on different occasions with regard to different issues.[25] On the one occasion when a conflict in guidance occurred, the apparent difference was resolved after about a week and was explained in terms of each 'sensitive' being unique as an individual and thereby attuning to different aspects of the one Divine—hence the *apparent* difference in guidance received.

The paradoxical situation at Findhorn where the notion of a spiritual élite was rejected but where the community life itself was run along autocratic lines with overall policy decision-making residing very firmly in the hands of Peter Caddy was resolved to the satisfaction of the leaders in a number of ways. First of all it was claimed that certain 'young souls' were not capable of exercising any significant decision-making ability. This was something they were expected to develop whilst they were at Findhorn. Second, the very practical justification was offered that in a community with a size of over a hundred it would be administratively impossible to have everyone exercising an equal voice in the policy-making procedure. Third, no contradiction was seen between the centralisation of power at Findhorn and the stated belief that each must find his own spiritual path. If a person did not like the life at Findhorn, then obviously he was more suited to a different spiritual path and he was expected to leave. The expulsion of dissidents and anyone who Peter decided did not fit in at Findhorn was one of the ways divisions and potential sources of conflict were dealt with, although this practice in itself could lead to conflict. Conceivably, as Findhorn grows in size this practice might increase along with an increased selectivity of recruits and the exposure of new members to an extended educational or socialization period. However, it would require a major change in the belief system if a scheme were ever introduced whereby potential recruits were required to proclaim their adherence to a detailed creed.

4   *Community v. New Age machine*

One of the problems that must be faced by any communal group which experiences a rapid growth in numbers and in range of activities is the danger of factionalisation developing within the community. As numbers increase the possibility of communication through constant face-to-face encounters between all the members diminishes. As the range of activities increases, so people become involved in different areas of communal life as the division of labour increases. Craftsmen can tend to interact primarily with other craftsmen, gardeners with other gardeners and so on. Furthermore, as the concern to develop a stable financial basis for the community through the business ventures increases along with the increased numbers, so less attention can be paid to the integration of new members into the community. They are no longer joining a small primary group but are joining a relatively large-scale organisation with a fairly complicated structure. Findhorn has had to face all these problems. Thus, a meeting was called for new members in July 1972 when over 75 people attended:[26]

> At the meeting it was expressed that more time and opportunity for social contact with other members of the community was needed . . . due to an apparent lack of social time for conversation and the postponement of college classes, the new members were having to integrate into the community almost

entirely through their own work patterns. A feeling of being a cog in a New Age machine was even talked about.

It is as a response to this problem that small discussion groups were started as a regular feature of life at Findhorn. In addition, the communal activities such as meals, 'fun nights' and sanctuary, the college classes and the outdoor activities such as rock-climbing and canoeing, and the monthly community meetings were considered as important means of bringing people together and countering the emergence of factional groups and individuals experiencing anomie. Furthermore, a weekly newsheet was started 'to bridge any communication difficulty within the community and to release a unifying energy, thus synthesising community activity'.[27]

The response of other religious groups to this kind of problem has been for the original community to give birth to new 'offspring' communities when numbers have risen to a particular level.[28] However, such a response brings with it another key problem faced by communal groups, the problem of succession and the replacement of key personnel.

5   *The problem of succession*

Given Findhorn's function as a training centre for the leaders of the New Age, it is accepted that many of the people, such as the Americans who occupy key organisational positions within the community, will leave the venture at some stage. Their departure could have a significant impact on the community. At Findhorn there was a complete faith that through the laws of manifestation replacements for key personnel would turn up at the right moment but it was repeatedly emphasised to members that in preparation for their day of departure each person must train a deputy who would be able to take over when they leave. Assuming that recruitment levels continue as they have done then one would expect that the replacement of the 'middle levels of management' should present no overwhelming difficulty in the future. When one turns attention to the higher level of Peter and Eileen then Weber's emphasis on the death of the original charismatic leader and its impact on the organisational structure and life of a religious group seems well founded. It is difficult to conceive of Findhorn having grown at the rate and in the manner it has done, without being split by dissension and conflict, without the organisational ability and energies of Peter Caddy and without Eileen's ability to contact God and thereby obtain a 'final reading' on almost any issue which arises. They themselves were aware of the key positions they occupied at Findhorn and, as has been remarked, it was this awareness which partly explained their concern to embark upon a process of decentralisation. Moreover, they had received guidance that one of the present members was to be trained as Peter's 'right hand man', presumably in the anticipation of Peter withdrawing to an extent from involvement in the day-to-day running of the community. However, it is one thing to prepare the way for a successor but it is a vastly different question whether that person will be able to command the same respect, willing obedience and love as the original charismatic leader when the latter is no longer around to lend his support. Ultimately Findhorn will have to confront this problem. All that can be said at the moment is that the present leaders themselves have no doubt that the right person will emerge at the right time so long as the eternal truth of man's oneness with God is recognised and they obey the 'rhythms' of this oneness.

Conclusion

In examining the ways in which Findhorn as a contemporary religious group has grown and responded to internal and external pressures and constraints that have been encountered in its ten years of existence, it has been emphasised that the 'transformation of Findhorn' has been facilitated by the flexibility of the belief system. It is this same flexibility which, amongst other things makes it virtually impossible to predict the future development of Findhorn. One thoughtful member of the community could only reply, 'anything could happen', when I asked him how he envisaged the future of the community. As with so many things at Findhorn, Divine support could be invoked for this prediction. In June 1971 David Spangler, in communication with a spiritual being called 'St Germain' received the following information:

I cannot portray clearly to you what you are moving into, but I assure you that it is there. I also say that each of you must learn to be free of the disciplines and training of the past when they cease to provide the proper power or energy to deal with the future. Be prepared in this centre for absolute reduction to the

very foundations of what you believe in, even to a point where
you may feel that nothing that you have believed in is correct.
Do not hold on to the past. Do not release yourself into chaos
either.

If a higher spiritual being cannot predict the future of Findhorn I
fail to see how a mere sociologist can be expected to either.

Postscript

After completing a first draft of this chapter, I sent a copy to
Findhorn for their comments. The reply I received in the spring of
1973 from Peter Caddy was that they were all surprised at how
accurately I had portrayed the tensions and stresses experienced at
the community (pat on the back for Andrew!), but that the situation had changed somewhat since my visit in 1972, and would I
care to return in order to look for myself? So it was that in April
1973 I returned once again to Findhorn.

The developments that had taken place illustrate one of the major
points of this book: that there is no one single necessary path along
which a community 'inevitably' must travel. Rather, the line of
development pursued by a communal group is one which it con-
structs itself in response to, and in anticipation of, new and emergent
situations and problems which the members see themselves as facing.
The manner in which the relevant members cope with new issues
and situations is influenced by the goals which they see themselves
as pursuing through the medium of communal living. The range of
available responses to new situations that the members define as
open to them is in turn significantly influenced by the flexibility of
their belief system. This factor has proved particularly important in
allowing the members at Findhorn the necessary freedom of man-
oeuvre to cope with the issues that have confronted them at each stage
in the life of the community. The usefulness of this flexibility was
also revealed in the developments that took place there during the
winter months of 1972–3.

The most obvious development brought to my notice on my
return was the fact that forty members, adults and children, had
left the community. Whilst the decision to leave was their own, they
had been 'helped' to realise that Findhorn was not the place for
them in the process of interviews and discussions with the 'élite' of

the community: Peter and Eileen Caddy, David Spangler and Myrtle Glines. The departure of these people had been accompanied by the closing-down of the art studios and craft workshops. This had been initiated by David Spangler in response to the problem of the actual and potential fragmentation of the community created by the membership in the community of people whose prime interest was in the arts and craft work rather than in the community life as a whole. The people in the craft studios, it was felt, were growing apart from the rest of the membership. Moreover it was also felt that they were too concerned with making the workshops economically viable as business enterprises. As a result, David decided, during Peter's absence in hospital, that the studios should be physically closed down for a period and, to counter the threatened break-up of the identity of the community, it was announced that the time had come for people to seriously examine their motives for living at Findhorn, to ask themselves whether the Centre was really the place for them, and to decide whether they wished to remain as members or not. It was made clear to people that anyone could discuss their situation with Peter, Eileen, David and Myrtle. For three days this group met with people to discuss their position in the community. Eventually a total of forty people, mainly drawn from those working in the studios, left. One group left to form a new, craft-oriented venture in the Lake District.

By the spring of 1973 the studios had been re-opened but, as one way to guard against the possibility of future fragmentation, steps had been begun to dismantle the legal company structure of the studios in order that they should become legally reintegrated into the overall legal structure of the Findhorn Trust. New people had also arrived and 'emerged' to take the place of those that had left. The general opinion of people seemed to be that whilst the departures represented a significant disruption in the on-going life of the community at the time, the aim of recapturing the 'togetherness' and sense of group identity had been attained.

Another change that had taken place involved the anticipated future role of Findhorn as a 'City of Light'. Again largely inspired by David Spangler, by spring 1973 it was anticipated that Findhorn was to become a 'University of Light' rather than a city. This apparent change in attitudes towards the future development of the venture resulted from the perception of an emerging 'problem area' of life at Findhorn. Again, the problem was most clearly seen by

David Spangler. As it was explained to me, Findhorn had begun to obtain a great deal of publicity. This was a relatively new situation which could be responded to in one of two ways. One possible response was the 'egoistic' one—that is, people could feel proud of what they themselves had achieved at Findhorn, experience a boost in their collective ego and bask in the reflected glory of the venture and content themselves with seeking to increase the glory and impressiveness of the community. The alternative, and more 'correct' response, according to David, was for the members to recognise their collective talents, recognise the achievements that had been made, but realise that such achievements and such talents were only an expression of the power and the talents of God. With such a realisation would come the awareness that Findhorn was only part of a whole, and that the important task for people in the community was not to serve Findhorn *per se* but to serve the whole, to seek to spread the message and the example of the New Age throughout the world. It was felt that the determination to make Findhorn into a City of Light represented an egoistic response to the new situation. The change to emphasise the future role of Findhorn as a University of Light represented the alternative response as moved and promoted by David Spangler, someone who had far greater contacts with the international network of spiritual and esoteric groups than anyone else at the community.

Other changes had also taken place since my previous visit, but what the examples referred to in this postscript indicate is the fact that by the time this book is published the scene at Findhorn, like the scene at the other ventures discussed, will have changed and been transformed as the members respond to new situations and emergent problems, constructing their own pathways towards their ideals.

Chapter 7

Conclusion

'Hasten to your own dreams.'

Whenever the subject of communes crops up in the mass media and arenas of public debate they are generally viewed as consisting of a single type. People tend to associate the word with the idea of a group of young, long-haired, drug-using artists and freaks 'doing their thing' in squalor out in the countryside. What I have tried to do in this book is to counter this image by portraying some of the variety and heterogeneity that exists in the commune scene in Britain.

The five projects considered are all very different from each other in many respects, although the differences should not blind one to the many similarities and comparisons that can be made between them. For instance, all had, by 1972, been in existence for over two years. Findhorn had in fact been in existence for a decade. Thus, apart from anything else, these ventures stand out from others in so far as they have not collapsed within a few months of their birth. In looking for reasons why these ventures have been successful in terms of their continued existence, when it appears that many other communes enjoy an extremely short life, one must look to the specific characteristics of each of them. Thus, it is extremely doubtful whether Findhorn could have grown and prospered as it has done without the charismatic leadership of Peter and Eileen Caddy. Similarly, without the commitment of David Horn it seems unlikely that the Kingsway Community could have managed to maintain itself as an on-going enterprise. The example of these two communities might convince people of the validity of the often-stated argument that for a commune to survive it needs a strong leadership. However, the examples of Newhaven, Shrubb Family and Postlip

K

stand as counters to this argument. In the case of these three, the crucial factor appears to have been their ability to obtain secure tenure of the property necessary for their respective ventures to thrive. Given security of tenure a commune can afford to experience crises of one sort or another, so long as there always remains at the end of the day a nucleus of people whose commitment to the idea and practice of communal living is unshaken.

In attempting to understand how these different groups have managed to stay the course for the length of time that they have done, however, one should really look to the kinds of 'rewards' that their members derive from membership which outweigh the undoubted 'costs' of living a communal mode of life. These rewards vary from one venture to the next. On the one hand, for the people at Postlip the rewards and advantages of communal living were seen primarily in terms of the possibility of living in property and surroundings which they would be unable to afford as separate family units. Likewise, the Newhaven dwellers were held to the commune largely because of the 'practical' advantages of sharing a large house with other young people, although the original aims of the founder group anticipated rewards in terms of promoting revolutionary change through the medium of the commune. For many of the people at Kingsway, the attraction of the community was undoubtedly seen in a similar manner—many of them would be without a roof over their heads if they had not found a home at the community. By way of contrast, for the people at Shrubb and Findhorn, and for certain members at Kingsway, the advantages of communal living, apart from the plain and simple fact that they enjoyed it, can only be understood in terms of their commitment to creating within the commune a new mode of life for themselves and others. Only by taking account of this genuine commitment to transform their own lives and ultimately the life of society in general can one understand their determination to live through and benefit from the various problems and hassles that accompany such forms of living.

Although many commentators both past and present have argued that a commune must have a strong leadership if it is to enjoy a lengthy life, the patterns of authority and decision-making revealed in these five experiments differ significantly. They vary not only in terms of the degree of membership participation in the decision-making process, but also in terms of the range of issues which are deemed relevant to the community as a whole and thereby require a communal decision. Thus, at one extreme even such an apparently minor issue as whether or not a new hair brush should be bought was deemed an appropriate matter for a community-wide decision by the Shrubb Family. On the other hand, at Postlip and Newhaven, few, if any, community-wide decisions were made and it was left up to the individual members to decide for themselves without reference to the others upon a whole range of matters. In between the two extremes, Findhorn and Kingsway were characterised by a certain degree of balance. Significant areas of life were deemed to be solely the concern of the individual, whilst other areas of life were considered to be of concern to the community as a whole. These communities were also the ones where formally articulated, 'written-down' rules were most apparent.

In similar fashion, the manner in which community decisions were arrived at varied from group to group. At Findhorn decision-making power rested firmly in the hands of Peter Caddy, although typically he would be following the guidance received by other key members of the Centre. Despite the attempts at decentralisation and delegation of powers at Findhorn, few of the members would claim that theirs was an experiment in living based upon practices of participatory democracy. At the other end of the scale, all community decisions at Shrubb Family were reached through a process which involved the full participation of all the members, a process facilitated by the limited size of the group. At Kingsway the theory was to involve all members in decision-making with the house-meeting as the sovereign body. In fact, and perhaps almost inevitably, given the size and the nature of the membership, a leading and determining role in decision making was frequently played by David Horn. In contrast, at Postlip and Newhaven, so restricted was the range of issues deemed relevant for decision-making at the community level that no standard practices or prodecures had emerged. At Postlip informal 'sounding out' of members' opinions was the key process in the 'emergence' of a decision, whilst life at Newhaven occasionally saw a house meeting at which everyone was able to participate in the decision-making process.

Just as the ventures considered here reveal different patterns of authority and decision making, they also reveal different degrees of what one might term 'communality'. At the one extreme, at Postlip, the members participated in few activities as a group. They lived

K*

in their separate dwelling areas, ate their meals separately, and pursued their own individual careers. The men came together to join in
the different ventures embarked upon by the Postlip Society, but
even here they tended to have areas of special interest which were
their particular preserves. At the other extreme, the members of
Shrubb Family shared the same house; although possessing their
individual bedrooms, they shared their meals together, and they also
worked together as a group on the various projects and enterprises
pursued by the commune. Life at Findhorn was also characterised
by a large number of communal leisure activities such as 'fun nights',
climbing expeditions and the like, in addition to the daily communal
gathering in the sanctuary and the members' participation in the
work of the studios and the other 'arms' of the community. At
Newhaven and Kingsway the communal activities were largely
confined to sharing the evening meal together, although at Kingsway
some attempt had been made to organise such group activities as a
weekly evening of table tennis and a weekly 'house activity' such as
a visit to the cinema. The communal activities at Newhaven were
essentially in the nature of friends going for a drink together, or
going out fell-walking for the day. That is, in participating in such
activities with other members of the commune, individuals would
probably reject any definition of their activities as 'commmunal'.
Rather, they defined such pastimes in terms of friends going out
together and doing the things that friends do together, rather than
in terms of themselves as a commune going out and doing together
the things that commune members do together. Thus, even their
participation in political activities was defined in terms of their
individual status as members of a particular political organisation
rather than in terms of their status as commune dwellers.

The arrangements that have evolved in the five groups concerning
finance and property reveal a similar range of variations. At the one
extreme, amongst the members of the Shrubb Family, the income
obtained from the fruit-loaf enterprise was pooled, new members
were expected to contribute their savings and capital into the
communal fund, and items such as their van were owned by the
commune rather than by individual members. Members also drew
their 'petty cash' requirements out of the communal purse. Incomes
were also pooled at Newhaven, with each member drawing out a set
amount for personal expenditure each week. However, whereas the
property that housed Shrubb Family was owned by all the members

in their capacity as members of the Shrubb Farm Company, the property at Edinburgh was owned, in legal terms at least, by the two original members who had raised the mortgage. Also, at Newhaven cars, clothes, records and such like remained the private property of the individual members although, as in Norfolk, expenditure on groceries, heating, etc. came out of the communal fund. It had been hoped that the Kingsway Community's finances would be organised along similar communal lines, but the actual practice appeared to fall somewhat short of this ideal. Certain members contributed their income into a communal pool out of which food, rent, rates, and fuel bills were paid, but others merely paid in a proportion of their income as 'rent'.

By way of contrast with this ideal at Kingsway, each family at Postlip retained responsibility for their own domestic expenses and only differed from the financial set-up of the standard nuclear family in that the rent they paid for their accommodation was paid to the Housing Association, whilst each family also paid a share of communal bills such as the rates. Private ownership and control of all personal property had been retained also. A small car for running the kids to school was one of the few items bought by members of the community together, and even in this case those without children did not contribute. At Findhorn, as at Postlip, members were not expected to contribute whatever capital they might possess into a communal fund (neither were they expected to relinquish ownership and control of their personal possessions). They were, however, expected to purchase their own living accommodation and possess sufficient resources to pay such things as the ground rent for their bungalows or caravans and contribute to the running expenses of the community. Those lacking such resources were paid a small amount each week to enable them to survive.

At least some of the growth and expansion at Findhorn can be explained in terms of their ability to obtain donations from various sources, including prospective members and new recruits. In contrast, Newhaven and Postlip received no financial support from such sources. Their income was obtained solely through the members selling their labour power in one form or another. Likewise, Kingsway relied mainly on the contributions made by members, although the community also received significant financial support and material assistance from outside donors and institutions. Shrubb Family, on the other hand, had to rely mainly on the income derived from the sale of their produce. A certain amount of cash was also obtained from visitors making contributions towards the expenses of the community, sources from which Findhorn also derived an income.

One could go on almost *ad infinitum* making these comparisons and pointing out the differences between the ventures, differences as regards such characteristics as their size, (from Findhorn with over 100 down to Shrubb Family with less than a dozen members), their dietary habits, (vegetarian at Shrubb Family and at Findhorn), the sexual division of roles, (very apparent at Findhorn and Postlip, not so apparent at Newhaven, Kingsway and Shrubb Family), and the development of communal economic enterprises, (non-existent at Newhaven, embryonic development at Kingsway and Postlip, limited development at Norfolk, and highly developed at Findhorn). Such comparisons would only emphasise the point: communes in Britain are not of a single type. They differ from each other along a whole range of dimensions, they embrace a variety of different types of people of different ages, sexes and from different social backgrounds.

At the same time, these different ventures in communal living share certain fundamental characteristics. Above all else, they represent attempts by people to develop patterns of living different from those conventionally considered 'normal' by the majority of folk. All of them are, in a very real sense, seeking to create alternatives to the largely unquestioned and taken-for-granted routines that guide and channel the lives of most of us. True, the contrast presented by life at Postlip with conventional nuclear family life might not appear to be very great to some people, but the fact remains that for the members themselves their venture does represent a significant break with their modes of existence prior to embarking upon the project.

However, the question remains: are these people doing anything more than creating their own private haven where they can enjoy their own particular version of the 'good life'? If one is to take seriously the protestations that certain commune members make about themselves as builders of a new social order, an alternative society, then surely they should break out of their communal cocoons and work for change in the 'real' world of working men and women? Surely one can say to the commune dwellers, particularly of the rural ventures, echoing the words of a member of the New-haven group: 'You are not going to change the world sitting on your arse in the countryside.' Are not commune members merely deluding themselves when they claim that they are out to change the world? Are they not merely fleeing from the world into their own private niches, merely mirroring in their own fashion the privatised response of many people in the conventional society to the problems that confront them—that of withdrawal—except that commune dwellers are withdrawing into the bosom of a commune rather than that of a nuclear family? Are not commune dwellers merely following the latest fad which is doomed to fade away like all fashions?

These are the charges and questions frequently levelled at those commune dwellers, particularly those living in rural communes, who claim that they are involved in a movement to transform the existing social order. They are most generally raised by members of the more conventional revolutionary socialist grouping. Their model of revolutionary change is based largely upon Marx's image of revolution in the nineteenth century. Theirs is a vision of a revolution being made by an impoverished working class rising to throw off its chains of oppression and exploitation under the 'correct' leadership. Someone once wrote of the revolutionaries of the nineteenth century:[1]

> The tradition of all dead generations weighs like a nightmare on the brain of the living, and just when they seem to be engaged in revolutionizing themselves and things, in creating something entirely new, precisely in such periods of revolutionary crisis they anxiously conjure up the spirits of the past to their service and borrow from them names, battle slogans and costumes in order to present the new scene of world history in this time honoured disguise and borrowed language. . . . The social revolution of the nineteenth century cannot draw its poetry from the past, but only from the future. It cannot begin with itself, before it has stripped off all superstition in regard to the past. . . . In order to arrive at its content, the revolution of the nineteenth century must let the dead bury their dead.

Perhaps a similar charge could be made against those revolutionaries of the twentieth century who are blind to new developments in both the social order and in revolutionary thinking and practice.

It has been one of the fundamental insights of libertarians and anarcho-pacifists that men create their own tyrants by granting them obedience; that all exploitation is based on the co-operation of the exploited; that there could be no exploitation if people refused to co-operate with the exploiter, for at some point in the relationship between exploiter and exploited there must come a point when, if the will of the exploiter is to prevail, the exploited must agree or consent to do that which is demanded of him or her. Similarly, it can be argued that the existing political, social and economic orders have their basis not so much in the armed might or economic power of ruling groups but in the fact that most people view the social world and their place in it as 'natural', as 'given', as something somehow apart from themselves about which they can do little except conform to the routines and habits that this social world appears to demand from them.

That is, although all social systems and institutional patterns have been created by men, can only persist so long as people consciously or unconsciously agree to play the part 'demanded' of them, and can only be changed through the purposive action of people, the bulk of people seem to have lost consciousness of this. Society, for the majority of its members, appears as something 'out there', comparable to the world of nature. The institutional arrangements, the patterns of human relations that characterise our social order, persist largely because they are taken for granted by most of society's members as the natural and only way that social life can be ordered. Not only do many folk have little conception of alternatives to the present order of things, they are unable to conceive of the actual possibility of any kind of purposive change brought about through the actions of 'ordinary people like themselves'.

Given this situation, it can be argued that the key process in any revolution involves people looking at their social arrangements and habitual routines with new eyes, a process through which people develop their awareness to the extent where they realise that very little in the social world is 'given', a process through which the consciousness of people is raised to the level where they realise that they, in concert with others, possess the ability to transform the social order, and that if they are ever to attain their ideals then they themselves must seek to change the world and not leave it to others to do it for them. The key process in any revolutionary period is the breakdown and collapse of the authority of the existing powers through the spread of disaffection from the *status quo* amongst the population, and the accompanying growth in their awareness of their world creating abilities, the development of new conceptions of what *ought* to be and the emergence of new styles of living and new forms of human relationships. This is the key anarchic process in any revolution, and typically it has been brought to an end in the past by the accession to control of centralised power of a single political group whose personnel are able to establish their own version of social order from above upon the masses below. Thus, whereas for many socialists the Russian Revolution proper was encapsulated in the seizure of power by the Bolsheviks, it can be argued that this, in fact, marked the *end* of the revolutionary process in Russia.

It follows from this perspective, then, that any attempt to inspire people with new visions, with new definitions of what is possible both for themselves as individuals and for society in general, any attempt to inspire people with new criteria by which to adjudge the quality of their lives and relationships with others, is a fundamental part of any revolutionary process. It is fundamental and basic in so far as it encourages people to transcend their habitual patterns of thinking, living, and relating with others and encourages them to demand the freedom to exercise their own wills unfettered by the straight-jackets imposed by conventional wisdom and the power of ruling groups. This is certainly a view echoed by a recent writer on the squatters movement in Britain, who has argued that,[2]

the most revolutionary thing in the world is to demonstrate to the disfranchised, alienated and therefore apathetic majority of people that they *can* act and win, and that they *can* run their own lives without rulers, politicians and their ilk.

It is true that particular communes can develop into virtual total institutions, prison-like in the restraints that are placed upon the freedom of action of their members. It is true that communes do not provide the necessary solutions and answers to the life problems of all people, perhaps the majority of people. This, I would argue is not particularly relevant. Thus, it would appear that many members of the Women's Liberation movement who, a few years ago, were looking to the commune as *the* answer to the oppression of women, have begun to question the suitability and desirability of communal living arrangements for all people, particularly women, who are estranged from the *status quo*. The development of such a critical attitude towards communes is a significant and positive development. From a position where radical women were rejecting the existing blueprint of the nuclear family and turning uncritically to the alternative blueprint presented by the commune, they have now moved on to search out and experiment with new forms of living and being, rejecting the blueprints of others, created to meet the needs of other people, in order to carry through their own projects.

In other words, communes can provide one answer to such life problems of modern existence as the isolation and loneliness of nuclear family life, the meaninglessness of the rat-race, the futility of consumerism, the boredom of nine till five work and so on. The important point, however, is not whether existing communes continue to persist or not. The important thing is whether or not the ideas that inspire such ventures are passed on and flourish amongst ever wider sections of the population. Thus, it could well happen that a generation from now all the ventures considered in this book will have ceased to exist. However it is conceivable that people will look back upon such experiments as marking a significant development in the kind of revolutionary process that I have been outlining. For, above all else, commune members are people who have begun to see through the fictions upon which our social order rests and who have sought to create their own modes of existence. The potential of this movement lies in the fact that through putting their bodies on the line, so to speak, through putting their ideals and beliefs into living practice, they can provide the spark to light the dreams of others and through their example can provide others with the courage to demand the right to decide for themselves the way they should lead their lives. It is this type of demand, crystallised in the stance of many communards, which lies at the heart of any true revolutionary process.

If our aim is not merely to change the system of ownership and control of wealth and property in society, but to transform all areas of life and in the process create a world where everyone is his own master, where we care for each other in a spirit of love and fraternity, where exploitation and hierarchical divisions between rulers and ruled in any area of life have no place—if such is our aim, then it can only be achieved through means which embody these ideals in the here-and-now, through people in all walks of life working to put these ideals into practice in their daily living. This is the message of the communes. Whether it will fall upon the ears of an audience too deeply entrenched in the *status quo* and their accustomed patterns of thinking and acting to respond, or whether the example of the communes and other allied groups will prove to represent the first stirrings that will herald widespread change, one cannot say. Nothing is inevitable. What one can say, however, is that the society of our dreams will never be attained unless we work to create it. In the words of Kenneth Patchen:

> Hasten to your own kind,
>   to your own dream,
>   to your own land,
> Hurry
> while there is still someone
> to go with you there . . .

Notes

1 Introduction

1 See Charles A. Reich, *The Greening of America*, Harmondsworth, Penguin Books, 1971.

2 See R. Lewis, *Outlaws of America: The Underground Press and its Context: Notes on a Cultural Revolution*, Harmondsworth, Penguin Books, 1972.

3 See Richard Fairfield, *Communes U.S.A., A Personal Tour*, Boston, Penguin Books, 1972, p. 3.

4 See T. Kelly, 'Communes in Japan', *Communes*, no. 31, February 1970.

5 See M. Mader, *The Kibbutz—an Introduction*, London, World Zionist Organisation, n.d., p. 2.

6 See S. Engert, 'Living now for the time after the revolution', *Peace News*, no. 1740, 31 October 1969, p. 8.

7 See P. Van Mensch, 'Something on the Dutch commune scene', *Communes*, no. 31, February 1970, pp. 10–11.

8 See Andrew Rigby, *Alternative Realities*, London, Routledge & Kegan Paul, 1973.

9 Laura Ross, 'The Newhaven Commune', *Eclectics*, no. 1, mark 2, October 1971, p. 11.

10 H. Blumer, 'Social Movements', pp. 8–29, in B. McLaughlin ed., *Studies in Social Movements*, New York, The Free Press, 1969, p. 8.

11 Keith Melville, *Communes in the Counter Culture*, New York, William Morrow, 1972, p. 16.

12 A. MacIntyre, *Secularization and Moral Change*, London, Oxford University Press, 1967, p. 12.

13 Fred Davis, 'Why all of us may be hippies someday', *Transaction*, no. 5, December 1967, pp. 14–15.

14 Correspondent to *Communes*, no. 37, March 1971, p. 21.

15 E. Goffman, 'The Moral career of the mental patient', pp. 88–98, in E. Rubington and M. S. Weinberg eds, *Deviance: The Interactionist Perspective*, New York, Macmillan, 1968, p. 89.

16 'Rochester Commune', *Arts Lab Newsletter*, March 1970, pp. 5–6.

17 Charles Nordhoff, *The Communistic Societies of the United States*, New York, Dover, 1966, pp. 411–12.

18   Vivian Estellachild, 'Hippie communes', pp. 40–3, *Woman, a Journal of Liberation*, ɫol. 2, no. 2, Winter 1971, p. 40.
19   Nordhoff, *op. cit.*, p. 410.
20   Quoted in W. H. G. Armytage, *Heavens Below: Utopian Experiments in England, 1560–1960*, London, Routledge & Kegan Paul, 1968, p. 23.
21   See Elia Katz, *Armed Love: Communal Living—Good or Bad?*, London, Blond & Briggs, 1972, pp. 191–3.

2   Newhaven: an activist commune

1   Ross, *op. cit.*, p. 11.

3   Shrubb Family: a self-actualising commune

1   Owen Thompson, 'Norfolk Commune', *Communes*, no. 33, June 1970, pp. 9–10.
2   See Ann Link, 'A directory of alternative work', *Peace News*, no. 1824, 18 June 1971.
3   *Communes*, no. 40, October 1972, pp. 17–19.
4   See Chapter 6 below.

4   Kingsway Community

1   *The Community Voice*, no. 1, February 1970.
2   This death was followed by a further tragedy the next day, as the following news item taken from the *Guardian*, 10 November 1972 reveals:

>   Spent £80 a week on drugs.
>   A woman heroin addict spent £80 a week on black market drugs, paid for by crime, and claimed she could forge any doctor's prescription in London, an inquest at Hammersmith was told yesterday. She was found dead from a huge barbiturate overdose the day after her boy friend died from chronic drug addiction, it was said.
>   Yesterday, two days after the coroner, Dr. John Burton, held the inquest on the boy friend, he recorded a verdict that Miss Constance Hughes, 21, took her own life. She had been living at the home of Dr. Michale Stok, at Strand Gardens, Grove Park Road, Chiswick, who told the inquest he had tried to cure her addiction.
>   Dr. Stok said: 'She had been charged with forging prescriptions, but she promised me she wouldn't forge my signature. There was no drug she couldn't get, she told me.
>   'She had been thrown out of a commune in Chiswick, and would not go to a clinic. She told me she spent £80 on drugs which she got from crime like pickpocketing,' said Dr. Stok. 'Her boy friend, *John Brown*, had died from drug addiction the day before her death.'

3 This point was made by David in a letter to me. He wrote, 'We are a departure from our recipe for a community as it has been circumstances alone that have driven people to us: only my wife and I came to it by choice. . . .'

4 Brian was learning to box in 1972, at least partly in order to be able to defend himself.

5 Louis Mendel, 'Kingsway Community', *Peace News*, no. 1855, 28 January 1972, p. 4.

5 Postlip Hall: a practical commune

1 Sandy McMillan, *Communes*, no. 37, March 1971, p. 11.

2 The unannounced visits of curious sightseers did cause some irritation for the members. I was told of one car-load who drove up to the front of the house, turned round, and were about to drive away when their exit was blocked by John. He asked the driver whether he could be of any assistance to them. 'No, we just came for a look,' was the reply. 'Oh, in that case do you mind telling me where you live then?' John asked. 'Why?' the perplexed driver retorted. 'So that I can come round and have a look at where you live,' came the reply. 'I think that's bloody rude,' said the driver. 'Well fuck off out of here, then,' concluded John. Exit one irate family man with his little horde in tow.

3 McMillan, *op. cit.*

4 See George Ineson, *Community Journey*, London, Sheed & Ward, 1956, for the story of the Taena Community.

5 Hydroponics is a system of growing plants in which the necessary nutrients are provided in a water solution by the grower, with the result that the plants can be grown in any sterile substance as their food is not derived from the soil. The practitioners of this method claim that the results are superior to those obtained through more conventional methods of horticulture.

6 See E. Lemert, 'Paranoia and the dynamics of exclusion,' *Sociometry*, 25 March 1962, pp. 2–25.

7 The fact that one member expressed the opinion that Chris's habit of inviting people to visit, only for him to go off and forget about them, was as bad as someone living at '23 Railway Cuttings' inviting people to visit and then forgetting about it, was indicative of the way the members saw the community: as something only marginally different from any block of separate dwelling places.

6 Centre of Light, Findhorn

1 Peter Caddy, *The Findhorn Story*, Findhorn Trust, 1969, n.p.

2 *Ibid.*

3 David Spangler, *New Age Energies and New Age Laws*, Findhorn Trust, 1970, n.p.

4   Sir George Trevelyan, in introduction to *The Findhorn Garden*, Findhorn Trust, 1969, p. 5.

5   See postscript below. By 1973 the emphasis on the future of Findhorn as a *City* of Light had changed to an emphasis on its future role as a *University* of Light.

6   Peter Caddy, *Moving into the New Age*, Findhorn Trust, 1969, p. 8.

7   *Transformation of Findhorn*, Findhorn Foundation, 1972, p. 35.

8   *Findhorn News*, March 1969, p. 2.

9   In fact, by 1973 this person had not joined in the full sense of purchasing living accommodation on the site. He still lived in his house in Findhorn.

10 *Transformation of Findhorn*, p. 14.

11 *Ibid.*, p. 7.

12 *Ibid.*, p. 26.

13 *Ibid.*, p. 33.

14 Spangler, *op. cit.*

15 See pamphlet, *New Policy for Mailing List*, Findhorn Foundation, 1972.

16 *Transformation of Findhorn*, p. 34.

17 *Findhorn and Finance*, Findhorn Foundation, 1972, n.p.

18 *Ibid.*

19 David Black, 'Whole within wholes', *Peace News*, no. 1855, January 1972, p. 6.

20 *Transformation of Findhorn*, p. 19.

21 Max Weber, *The Theory of Social and Economic Organisation*, translated by A. M. Henderson and Talcott Parsons, edited with an introduction by Talcott Parsons, London, Collier-Macmillan, 1966, p. 362.

22 *Ibid.*, p. 369.

23 See David Spangler, *The Vision of Findhorn in World Transformation*, Findhorn Trust and the Universal Foundation, 1971.

24 *Transformation of Findhorn*, pp. 8–9.

25 Typically, David Spangler would obtain guidance on broad issues and general principles. Elixer obtained guidance on practical and immediate matters requiring specific guidance.

26 *Weekly News*, no. 9, 22 July 1972.

27 *Weekly News*, no. 1, 26 May 1972.

28 This has been the practice of such groups as the Hutterites. See V. Peters, *All Things Common: the Hutterian Way of Life*, University of Minnesota Press, 1965.

7   Conclusion

1   Karl Marx, *The Eighteenth Brumaire of Louis Bonaparte*, quoted in *Listen Marxist*, a pamphlet printed by Leeds Anarchist Group, n.d., pp. 1–2. The article appeared originally in the New York anarchist magazine *Anarchos*, May 1969.

2   Ron Bailey, *The Squatters*, Harmondsworth, Penguin Books, 1973, p. 139.

Index